The New Nihilism

The New Nihilism

The Existential Crisis of Our Time

Costantino Esposito

University of Notre Dame Press

Notre Dame, Indiana

Published in the United States of America

Library of Congress Control Number: 2024943289

ISBN: 978-0-268-20799-1 (Hardback)
ISBN: 978-0-268-20798-4 (WebPDF)
ISBN: 978-0-268-20801-1 (Epub3)

And take upon's the mystery of things,

As if we were God's spies

—W. Shakespeare, *King Lear*, act 5, scene 3

CONTENTS

PREFACE

The remote occasion from which the idea of this book was born was a meeting with Andrea Monda, the director of *L'Osservatore Romano*, who some time before had invited me to collaborate with the historic Vatican newspaper, leaving me complete freedom and unrestrainedness in choosing themes and problems for my contributions.

In response to his invitation, my proposal was to focus on contemporary nihilism—in a series of interventions appearing periodically and linked together as a single path. The working hypothesis that supported this proposal arose from a discovery that has become increasingly clear and documented over the past few years. And this not only as I have followed the current cultural, scientific, and philosophical debates but also and especially as I have followed—so to speak, "in the field"—the phenomenon "nihilism" through the encounter and relationship with my students at the University of Bari. The hypothesis was this: after having exploded in titanic and iconoclastic form with Nietzsche in the passage from the nineteenth to twentieth centuries, nihilism had been transformed, little by little during the twentieth century, from a "pathology" to the "physiology" of the dominant culture in the societies of the advanced West (and from here to many parts of the globe). Finally, in our time, nihilism seemed to have completely won, and therefore no longer to constitute a "problem," but rather an obvious condition shared globally. On the contrary, observing the scene better, it seemed to me that just in these last years nihilism had become an open question again. Thanks to its critique of idols, the questions that nihilism had by now declared impossible—such as the question on the ultimate meaning of oneself and of reality, on the truth of the ego and of history, on our relationship with the infinite, and so on—were becoming once again possible, reasonable, burning. Paradoxically, nihilism today no longer seems to consist—as in its classical form—in a loss of values and ideals, but rather in the emergence of an irreducible need. There are fewer ideological protections: the need is more naked, and therefore much more demanding. It has no more cover, and therefore, nihilism can paradoxically be a *chance*.

The style of my reflections—ten episodes, appearing every fifteen days, from January 15 to May 19, 2020, under the title "Chronicles from Nihilism"—was conceived from the beginning as a sort of reportage, in which the observer or the traveler could note cues, problems, perspectives, new phenomena, questions that disturb. The method for this journey was observing—without prejudice, indeed with a basic sympathy—social phenomena and poetic voices, television series and philosophical and scientific visions, ethical problems and aesthetic experiences. Each reportage does not pretend to analytically exhaust the problem, but aims above all at *making it visible*, trying to identify with the less obvious forms in which the meaning of being returns to emerge as a new question—or an old one, but relived. The place where this happens is found to be precisely in some of the most critical points in which it seemed that meaning was impossible, and where instead, in an unexpected or paradoxical way, it reemerged, showing in human experience points of resistance or factors "irreducible" to any reductionism.

To this initial motivation was added, in the course of the work, a further reason for interest, namely the outbreak of the COVID-19 pandemic, with the consequent arrest of public life and the radical questioning of attitudes, practices, and habitual perspectives. This pandemic also broke into my "Chronicles," giving me a further opportunity to see, almost in real time, the vital questions reemerge in the face of a nihilism that showed itself no longer up to the task of intercepting and resolving the problem that "is" the life of human beings in the contemporary world. In other words, it allowed me to verify more radically my initial hypothesis: at some significant point in the existence of people and society, the overcoming of nihilism had already begun. It may take a long time, or a very long time; we don't know; but in any case it has already begun.

But the story of the book does not end here. At the end of my column in *L'Osservatore*, the publisher Carocci of Rome, in the person of its editorial director, Gianluca Mori, proposed publishing the ten articles together. He asked me, however, to considerably expand the texts of the articles that had already appeared, and to write other chapters that would make the horizon of the investigation more articulate, documented, and meditated upon. The result was a volume of eighteen chapters, designed with many angles or perspectives from which to see and listen to the phenomenon under discussion. The trajectory continued with the Spanish edition, to which a text dedicated to the television series *Euphoria* was added in the meantime.

Finally, with the American edition that I present here, the text has been significantly integrated with an extensive introduction, which proposes a sort of "cartography" of the main trends of the phenomenon of nihilism and its multifaceted meaning in the philosophical and cultural debate of recent years, with particular reference to the axis between Europe and the USA. Also for this American edition, a conclusion has been purposely written, which resumes the path taken in the book by highlighting the problems that contemporary nihilism forces us to reopen and recognize as "irreducible" issues, proposing a possible way to continue the crossing and perhaps try to go beyond the nihilism of our time from within.

Some basic themes, like continuous threads, unravel among the various chapters. Sometimes they are taken up again, or return through different cases and contexts of observation; other times they are intertwined with other threads. The essential thing, however, is to always keep in mind the phenomenon studied as an event in motion: in this horizon, even the individual details can take on their most interesting meaning. As far as writing is concerned, my attempt was to combine the rapidity and essentiality of a journalistic piece with the opening of broader perspectives of philosophical investigation—without limiting myself, however, to simply juxtaposing the two approaches, trying to intercept the "epochal" scope that is often hidden in the details of the cultural, anthropological, and social experience of our time and at the same time verifying in the data of daily experience the fundamental questions of our being in the world.

The book has no footnotes, only bibliographic references to works cited or used for each chapter, at the end of the book. Finally, I would like to warmly thank Dr. Antonio Lombardi for his intelligent and generous help in preparing the American edition of the book.

CHAPTER ONE

INTRODUCTION TO THE AMERICAN EDITION

For a Cartography of the Nihilism of Our Time

The term "nihilism," especially when it is used to denote a philosophical trend, a sociocultural phenomenon, or an anthropological dimension, is always in danger of meaning too much or having a confused meaning. Certainly it has had its own distinct history as a philosophical and literary category, starting at least with Friedrich H. Jacobi's critique of Johann G. Fichte's idealistic rationalism, through the real existential experiences of nihilism offered by the novels of Ivan S. Turgenev and Fyodor Dostoyevsky, to the capital theorizing—in the ontological, theological and psychological sense—of Friedrich Nietzsche and Martin Heidegger, along with Ernst Jünger and Albert Camus. This is only to name a few of the most significant authors who have "engaged" with nihilism. From the outset, these interpreters have provided a theoretical definition and a practical description of the nihilist phenomenon in its many implications; at the same time they have also proposed a verification of the legitimacy of its claims and its possible developments. For nihilism could never be spoken of as a mere fact or as a mere tendency of thought, because its very nature consists in posing a problem, or rather in being a problem: more specifically a problem without a solution. It in fact arose and developed as a radical critique of the conceptual, cultural, religious, and political arrangements of a world considered outdated and inadequate to the most urgent instances of life, or as an attempt to overturn the principles of a tradition considered decayed and now inert. But along with this, nihilism has proved itself always or mostly incapable of giving an adequate answer to its lack: "Nihilism: the aim is lacking; 'why?' finds no answer," according to the icastic formula of Nietzsche (*Will to Power*). It is unable to resolve his most radical question, that of an ultimate sense of self and world. But this story is only the "prequel" to our story, to the nihilism of our time.

This book starts from a precise thesis, namely, that in the course of a "long" century, nihilism has been radically transformed: from being an acute crisis of thought and of the human condition—a crisis that carried within itself the expectation of redemption, that is, of an answer to the most proper need of reason and of the human heart—it has been turned upside down into the solution of its own crisis. Discovering that the ultimate meaning of the real eludes us, that the traditional image of the world has waned, has led to the conclusion that there is no possible answer to this need. But this in turn has led to weakening the very question of meaning, and finally to "burning it out," as if there was no oxygen left to breathe. If an answer that lives up to our questioning is unlikely, and even ruled out, why should we continue to ask the question? As I will try to document in the following chapters, precisely when the crisis is no longer understood as the need and possibility of a new perspective, but is simply reversed in its solution—that is, when the problem of ultimate meaning is solved by affirming the impossibility of this meaning—precisely then it paradoxically loses its radicality. The crisis then ceases to be scabrous and becomes tranquilizing; it divests itself of the tone of revolt to assume that of normalization. This is why nihilism ultimately won, while dampening its most burning or irreducible questions: precisely those that appeared to be without solution.

Two things seem to be, in our time, the outcomes of this strange "victory." First, nihilism, in its weak form, has become a "canon," a kind of shared style of thinking, according to which it would be an incorrect claim—in a philosophical and at the same time political sense—to believe that there is a "true" sense of the world. And this across the most diverse cultural positions, even those that are not overtly "nihilist"—something like the Hegelian Zeitgeist, the "spirit of the time" in which everyone, regardless of individual options, finds himself or herself living and thinking (more on this in the following pages). Second, the normalization process that nihilism has gone through has entailed—and still entails—a kind of "mourning" for the loss of an ultimate or irreducible meaning of the real. And this has led in many instances, in the philosophical and scientific debate of our time, to a loss of consistency of the very "I" that demands meaning. In short, everything would tend to be reducible to a natural process or cultural construction.

It is worthwhile then, as an introduction to our journey, to try to identify some of the current perspectives on nihilism (or postnihilism), mapping out the problems and also the solutions that its victory—which is at the same time its weakening—has disseminated in the thought and culture of our time. This kind of cartography may come in handy as we try to orient ourselves on the path we will attempt in the following chapters, to clarify the multiple meanings of the term "nihilism," to highlight and try to cross its boundaries.

Nihilism as Emancipation

The "normalized" nihilism I am talking about is no longer Nietzsche's "active nihilism," which intended to radically question the truths of traditional metaphysics and morality (I will return to this). Rather, it is subsequent to what Gianni Vattimo has called "the Heidegger Effect," namely, "the involvement of the interpreter in the event, in the game of interpretation—that in Nietzsche was announced but then was forgotten by him" (Vattimo, *Of Reality*). But what does it mean for Vattimo that the nihilism of our time is a "post-Heideggerian" nihilism? In it, Nietzsche's iconoclastic and demolishing gesture is transformed into "hermeneutic" practice in the ongoing exercise of interpretation. In other words, the critique of the traditional idea of "reality" or "given" as metaphysical substance or "presence" is transvalued into a sociocultural construction. More importantly, the last "metaphysical" remnants present in the Nietzschean doctrines of the will to power and the eternal return of the equal are also abandoned. On the other hand, Vattimo also identifies another movement, apparently contrary to the first, whereby the overcoming of metaphysics proposed by Heidegger is accomplished in a return to Nietzsche, and his idea of a nihilism is realized through the figure and practice of the "beyond-man." Against all reactionary interpretations, the image of a "liberator" Nietzsche is proposed here (and from the left!): the "beyond-man" is not a man to the nth power, the ruler of tomorrow envisioned by National Socialism, but rather the "comedian" and the "free creator of symbols" who despises all forms of domination, metaphysics, and traditional morality (Vattimo, *Il soggetto e la maschera*).

If hermeneutics thus proposes itself as a "weak thought" or "post-metaphysical" thought, in which being is given only as historical and finite "happening," precisely in this it reveals its "nihilist vocation" (Vattimo, *Beyond Interpretation*). As a hermeneutic nihilism, weak thought asserts that knowing truth no longer means defining a necessary ("logical") relation between a ground and a grounded, but practicing the free ("rhetorical") relation between certain linguistic and social rules and their cultural products. This would in a sense be an obligatory path, demanded by our time as the time of a "transparent," increasingly "public" and publicized, antiauthoritarian, post—or rather ultra—modern society, aimed at the self-construction of individuals on the basis of the claim of their rights. But in the globalized communication society, all the disorientation that inevitably (but positively) accompanies the possibility of relating to all points of view at once emerges. The overflowing amount of information and positions accessible through the mass media and the web is part of the project of weak thinking: "It is precisely in this relative 'chaos' that our hopes for emancipation reside" (Vattimo, *Transparent Society*, it. 11). It is precisely here that the Nietzschean announcement of the beyond-man remains, according to Vattimo, the paradigm of the possibility of living—without neurosis—the oscillation between belonging (to a history, to a tradition) and disorientation (the weakening of my point of view in that of others, and vice versa).

This social secularization of values does not simply lead to the relativism and cynicism typical of the transaction of special interests. On the contrary (at least in Vattimo's intentions) in a society in which we take leave of the absolutist "domination" of truth, it becomes possible to rediscover the regime of "charity" and "pietas." Even Christianity itself, with its strong idea of a God who lowers himself and finally annihilates himself in the human (kenosis), would paradoxically fulfill itself precisely by "weakening" itself in nihilism. And the latter constitutes the only possible "hermeneutical" truth of Christianity, and with it of the whole tradition of Western thought, which is still indebted to its Christian sources.

Nihilism as Voluntarism and Anarchism

The nexus just examined of nihilism and emancipation is actually neither new nor exclusive to our time: indeed, it can be said that the emancipatory dimension has always been present from the beginning in the history of the nihilistic phenomenon. Deconstruction for liberation. Of course, the meaning and especially the direction with which this emancipation has been understood changes from time to time. For example, in weak hermeneutics, or so-called postmodernism, we encounter a very different kind of emancipation, if not opposed to the subversive and "titanic" emancipation of nineteenth-century Russian nihilism, which, as Michael Allen Gillespie has written, "was characterized by a longing for the Promethean, for a new kind of human being who rises above the level of humanity in search of autonomy" (*Nihilism before Nietzsche*).

But to understand what is happening in our time one must go even further back in history. Following Gillespie's suggestion again, it can be observed that nihilism did not arise, as Nietzsche would have it, from the "death of God," but well before, and in a purely theological context: it arose when the idea of God's absolute will was dissolved from any connection with rationality and when the divine omnipotence came to be thought of (e.g., in William of Ockham and the Franciscan School) as a decision that in principle can go beyond (and even against) the rational order of the world. In the course of modern thought—from Descartes to Fichte and Romanticism—this idea will be secularized to a "divinized" conception of man, capable of promethean opposition to the gods. According to Gillespie, this idea of superhumanity is fundamental not only to understanding the thought of the Russian nihilists but also to finding a proper understanding and an adequate "solution" to today's nihilism. For if it all began with a gesture of pure anthropological voluntarism (born, as noted above, out of the secularization of the theological idea of *potentia Dei absoluta*), then it will be necessary to thoroughly rethink the use of the human will and take, as it were, a "step back" from the option of voluntarism. It is on the latter that, alongside the Nietzschean will to power, the "anarchy" of the Russian nihilists depends. Let us think of Evgenij Bazarov, the protagonist of Turgenev's *Fathers and Sons*, who rejects the principles of his fathers' culture, seen as unbearable dogmas. And even more, let us think of two emblematic characters created by Dostoyevsky, such as Aleksej Kirillov (*The Demons*) and Ivan from *The Brothers Karamazov*: the former affirms an idea of freedom as absolute self-determination of the human being, whose extreme test would be his own self-suppression; the latter denies the existence of a God who is unbearable, on account of the absurdity of evil and innocent pain in the world.

But also on the horizon of contemporary thought we can register—this time after Nietzsche and Heidegger—an "anarchist" outcome of the emancipatory potential proper to nihilism. This is what emerges from Reiner Schürmann's thesis that the "event" character proper to being—no longer a substantial presence but a historical happening in the socio-linguistic sense—has led to the "closure" of the history of metaphysics, and thus to a finally anarchist conception of origin. "Anarchic" in the sense of being destitute of the claim to be valid as a principle for the life and action of human beings and societies. Such absence of the "principle," with the consequent disappearance of principles, realized along the path of modern philosophy, should by no means be understood, however, in a negative sense, as a loss. Rather it suggests (echoing a distant echo of the medieval Dominican Meister Eckhart) a "living without why," a "practical a priori" that does not intend to cling to conditions, motives, or ultimate foundations (Schürmann, *Heidegger on Being and Acting*). This would be nothing more than the contemporary translation of that lack of the why, by which Nietzsche defined nihilism. We lack the "why?" not occasionally, but ontologically, in that being itself "is" without principle, or more precisely happens precisely *because* it is without a why. Existence is not grounded in any cause or principle that precedes it. On the contrary, it is a praxis from which ends and principles arise from time to time. Nihilism then, paradoxically, is no longer a weakening or loss of being, but the most proper meaning of being. Anarchy thus becomes the new nihilistic "principle" of reality.

Nihilism as Pragmatism and the "Creation" of Meaning

The precedence of the practical over the theoretical is basically the (neo-)pragmatist soul of today's nihilism: thought is "weak" because it depends on our sense-making practices. In other words, thought no longer has to "attest" to anything, but has to "process" everything, through the endless game of discourses and interpretations. Again, the idea that realized nihilism is no longer a merely destructive but properly "constructive" or "constructivist" phenomenon is taken up, directly or indirectly. Only now this no longer implies the claim of positing new values to replace the old ones, but rather pursues the simple "liberation" from all reference to really existing metaphysical presuppositions, and also challenges the claim that our mind contains within itself the formal conditions for representing the world as it is in itself, outside of us. Our being in the world is not of the cognitivist type but of the precisely "pragmatist" type.

In this perspective it is once again Heidegger's thought that offers an essential point of orientation: the overcoming of the "modern" subject must lead to an ontological reformulation of the human being, the prototype of which could be precisely the Heideggerian *Dasein*. The latter is no longer based on a "theory" of the mind, because on the contrary any theory is made possible by a process of understanding the sense of self and the world that actually happens, from time to time, in the vital, cultural and social context in which each of us is always embedded. Decisive in this regard has been Hubert L. Dreyfus's attempt to develop a pragmatist interpretation of Heidegger's *Being and Time*. Heidegger, according to Dreyfus, "introduces the idea that the shared everyday skills, discriminations, and practices into which we are socialized provide the conditions necessary for people to pick out objects, to understand themselves as subjects, and, generally, to make sense of the world and of their lives. He then argues that these practices can function only if they remain in the background." And this does not at all mean giving up the plane of "being" over that of "doing" or "acting," but recognizing the "nonexplicable background that enables us to make sense of things" and that Heidegger calls precisely "the understanding of being" (Dreyfus, *Being-in-the-World*). This "commonsense background" can never be translated into the theoretical clarity of a formal model (John Searle would say that it is "invisible to Intentionality as the eye which sees is invisible to itself") and thus remains irreducible to the "computer model of the mind." But it is precisely here that theoretical nihilism, that is, the deconstruction of formal models to explain our being in the world, spills over into a hermeneutic constructivism—not in the weak form of a relativistic perspectivism, but in the epistemologically more conscious form of a true "pragmatism." To understand how things "are" and how I myself "am," I cannot and must not retreat "from everyday practical concern," because in these "practices" my pretheoretical, everyday understanding of being produces the sense of being. In this sense Dreyfus can claim that "Heidegger can be viewed as radicalizing the insights already contained in the writings of such pragmatists as Nietzsche, Peirce, James, and Dewey."

This "ontological" version of pragmatism has also been accompanied by a softer or more liberal, in short, more "urbanized" version, according to the image that Jürgen Habermas once used to define Gadamer's hermeneutics versus Heidegger's "provincial" (or peasant) ontology. An author such as Richard Rorty, for example, was instrumental in urbanizing the emerging pragmatist trend between the nineteenth and twentieth centuries in America and Europe by tracing its epistemological claims back to the rules of good "conversation" in society. In this view, philosophy itself is to be conceived "only" as a literary genre, which merely provides a description of different ways of saying the world: a "saying" that neither finds nor expresses the world as it "is," but rather "makes it be." For this very reason, a finally postphilosophical culture must accept that "there is nothing deep down inside us except what we have put there ourselves, no criterion that we have not created in the course of creating a practice, no standard of rationality that is not an appeal to such a criterion, no rigorous argumentation that is not obedience to our own conventions" (Rorty, *Consequences of Pragmatism*). It is the "democratic" potential of this total absence of predetermined essentialist-type criteria that, according to Rorty, the old pragmatists James and Dewey teach Nietzsche and Heidegger: there is no "being" of things, be it that of the will to power or of the event (*Ereignis*), but only our "doing them." This would have the advantage of leading us to a sympathetic, charitable, and ironic attitude toward reality and people, because it means that we no longer give predetermined orders in the name of which we can legitimately resort to any kind of coercion. As in any polite, proper, and pleasant bourgeois conversation, "if we do our best with our peers, we need not worry about answering to any other norms, nor to the world" (Rorty, "Response to J. McDowell"). This is why democracy (a living together no longer burdened by the weight of truth) can do more than philosophy (in the traditional foundational sense) can do.

Allow me a digression in this regard. Here come to mind the extraordinary "conversation pieces" painted in eighteenth-century England by an artist such as William Hogarth, in which a group of family or friends, or participants in a common activity or game, discuss among themselves in a relaxed, informal manner steeped in politeness, or, closer to home, the scenes in the many films depicting the charming levity and pleasant buzz of an upscale party in affluent Manhattan. Of course, in both cases the mise-en-scène leads one to suspect that, behind the perfect looseness of human relations and the agreement of individuals, there is a backstory or unspokenness of contrasts and disagreements, perhaps at that moment suspended and neutralized in the rules of being in society. But in any case, we would not be reminded of one of the disturbing "Black Paintings" (*Pinturas negras*) of the late Goya (1819–23) preserved at the Prado Museum or, to take up the analogy again, Stanley Kubrick's unforgettable, terrible film *A Clockwork Orange* (1971) or Roman Polański's *Carnage* (2011).

Returning to Rorty. He too would actually be reluctant to define his own perspective as "nihilistic," preferring labels such as "antifoundationalism," "anti-essentialism," or "anti-platonism." The term "nihilism" appears to him to be burdened with a negative existential connotation, whereas ironic and liberal philosophy must be, as he argues, "edifying": that is, a thought that, analogous to what Gadamer did in Europe, replaces the concept of "knowledge" with that of Bildung (which Rorty translates precisely as "edification"). The desire for the true must be succeeded by the desire for edification: "the attempt to prevent conversation from degenerating into inquiry, into a research program" (*Philosophy and the Mirror of Nature*). The purpose of "edifying philosophy" is to keep the conversation alive, opening up new spaces for dialogue and establishing novel connections between areas of discourse, without falling into the temptation of finding objective truth in it. This is why Rorty himself has at times defended nihilism against the accusations of those, such as Stanley Rosen, who saw in it a fall into a condition of meaninglessness and lack of justification of practices, because of Western thought's renunciation of the aspiration for truth. According to Rorty—who states here that he is speaking, precisely, "on behalf of the nihilist"—there is not necessarily a connection between the two; that is, one should not make the mistake of confusing "despair over the success of the Platonic project and despair over human life" (review of *Nihilism*, by Stanley Rosen).

Man living in a posttrue world is not for this reason condemned to live an empty and meaningless existence: rather, the waning of the myth of the correspondence of mind and reality, with the consequent crisis of knowledge understood as a "mirror of nature," entails the possibility of thinking philosophy in the sense of *self-construction* and self-enlargement: an enrichment of one's perspectives, which is opposed to the self-satisfaction of the old "systematic thinking" and is realized in an interpretive circle that is never closed; this self-construction is a "poietic" task in which art and literature can succeed better than philosophy, and imagination better than reason. Rortyan pragmatism is essentially hermeneutic in character; or as we might also say, it is a form of "nihilistic liberalism." Admittedly, this perspective is always tempted to yield to skepticism about truth and to resolve itself into mere sociocultural constructivism; in its depths, however, there is a vein of awe for what is new in reality, or rather for the newness that we ourselves can "make" of reality: "Great systematic philosophers, like great scientists, build for eternity. Great edifying philosophers destroy for the sake of their own generation. Systematic philosophers want to put their subject on the secure path of a science. Edifying philosophers want to keep space open for the sense of wonder which poets can sometimes cause—wonder that there is something new under the sun" (Rorty, *Philosophy and the Mirror of Nature*).

Nihilism as Secularization

In its most widespread sociocultural sense, nihilism is generally narrated as a "postmodern" ideology. This stems from its tendency to close accounts and do away with the great "narratives" of the twentieth century, that is, the theories that predetermined the true meaning of reality and history, incurring more often than not totalitarian outcomes. And indeed, it is precisely this disbelief in the ideological metanarratives inherited from modernity that, according to Jean-François Lyotard, characterizes the "postmodern condition." As postmodern, nihilism is understood—for better or worse—as a disenfranchisement from all discourses that want to speak about the ultimate "truth" of the world, history, and human existence. Among these discourses, often accused of being exclusionary and violent, a prominent role is naturally played by the "religious" discourse; indeed, it is precisely in reference to the latter that it is usual to link nihilism to the phenomenon of "secularization." In the "secular age" (a phrase used in the title of a seminal essay published by Charles Taylor in 2007) there is a gradual weakening and loss of incidence of faith in God and religious beliefs in the institutions and common practices of postmodern societies, which are no longer held together by the link with a transcendent reality. The consequence is there for all to see: a physiological decrease in the participation of the faithful in religious rites and institutions. However—and this is the most interesting side of the phenomenon—there is also a paradigm shift in the very subjective "conditions" of belief. These conditions are no longer guaranteed by a shared cultural tradition, and thus become problematic in a twofold sense: first, religious faith is systematically subjected to critique and is no longer understood as a universal rule but as a particular option; second, then, precisely as an alternative to the "secular option," faith requires a verification and reconquest of its personal motivations and cultural reasons.

In its—let us call it—"negative" side, secularization thus implies the progressive distrust of any reference to transcendence, a distrust that culminates in the "death of God," which then saw the large-scale rise of atheism in Western countries. In this sense, secularization would coincide with what Max Weber called the "disenchantment of the world" and what Taylor calls a "subtractive" account of secularization: "these stories of modernity in general, and secularity in particular, which explain them by human beings having lost, or sloughed off, or liberated themselves from certain earlier, confining horizons, or illusions, or limitations of knowledge" (Taylor, *Secular Age*). Taylor himself thought it is reductive to say that a society is secularized only because the institutions of today's states are no longer closely tied to religious rituals and codes ("public spaces . . . have been allegedly emptied of God, or of any reference to ultimate reality"), or because people no longer go to church or pray. If it were only that, secularization would have to be understood—and this is a widely held view—as an inevitable loss of transcendence and the definitive establishment of an "immanent frame" within which the lives of people and societies would be enclosed. But for Taylor things cannot be simplified in these terms; secularization is not a "neutral" process, like the irreversible decay of previous forms of life and beliefs, and therefore should not be seen as an inevitable and necessary loss. If we accepted this version, we would have to say that after the "death of God," "you can't be fully with the modern age and still believe in God. Or alternatively, if you still believe, then you have reservations, you are at last partly, and perhaps covertly, some kind of adversary."

The question remains, therefore, whether the secular age depends only on a "subtraction" of forms and visions of the past, or whether it carries within itself its own possibility, a specific potential for spiritual self-understanding. The understanding of self and the world typical of our time is "secularized" not only and not so much because it derives from the impossibility of drawing on the ancient resources of meaning but also and *especially* because it constitutes a new, specific, and original way of posing the problem of meaning. There is a "sense" of secularization that is not necessarily the enemy of spirituality: today faith is one option among others, certainly, but this means that those who embrace it can choose it reflexively and not necessarily inherit it passively. Indeed, such a choice may even be more sincere, because it is not taken for granted as it once was. According to Taylor, the transition to a secularized society does not coincide with the simple fact that belief in God has waned, but rather with the fact that "Belief in God is no longer axiomatic." This calls precisely for freer personal choice and new ethical options. Even religion is not doomed to irreversible decline, but is now faced with a new challenge: to understand what in it resists the loss of traditional moral systems, and thus how new horizons of meaning can be opened up not simply "beyond" the *immanent frame*, but to some extent from within it and through it. And here we cannot fail to refer to the interesting, exquisitely "theological" approach to the phenomenon and challenges of secularization proposed by Anglican John Milbank, for whom in secular society there still remain traces of the ancient theological categories now secularized, which, albeit anonymously, animate and direct the philosophical categories themselves from within.

To recognize, therefore, the "positive" sense of secularization is to realize an original path for the modern individual, not in spite of, but precisely insofar as he is marked by an "exclusive humanism"; that is, he no longer perceives as an "obligation" reference to something greater than himself. Such an individual has as his overriding perspective the affirmation of his freedom and rights, not only in a negative sense (self-determination) but also and especially in a positive sense, as motivated assent and lived adherence to that which enables him to be himself and to flourish humanly. Even the possible transcendent sense of the world can be regained, on this path, not by tradition but by freedom. If the meaning offered by faith and religion has waned because it is felt to be detached from the perception of individual freedom and the processes of social liberation, now truth can once again become interesting to the people of our time precisely through and by virtue of the freedom of individuals.

It is no accident that for some years now we have been talking about multicultural and multiethnic societies as "postsecular" societies. In them one must always admit, in principle as well as, of course, in fact, the possibility that the motivations for civil coexistence and for the constitutional order of the state itself may be drawn from prestate or extrastate experiences, in particular from "religious" experiences (as became clear in the 2004 public dialogue between two such outstanding figures as the then Cardinal Joseph Ratzinger and Jürgen Habermas). Secularism thus does not appear to be the ultimate "fate" of nihilism.

Nihilism as Reenchantment of the World

At the descriptive level, secularization certainly constitutes an essential factor of nihilism. However, we have seen that it should not be hastily identified with a "disenchantment" of the world. Taylor himself emphasizes the fact that in the secularized world people have spiritual experiences and choose forms of life marked by an intuition of "fullness" or a feeling of "reverence" (which echoes the *Achtung*, respect for the moral law mentioned by Kant), but also devotion or awe. Unlike in the earlier era, however, these experiences do not necessarily or primarily address themselves to a transcendent reality, but are realized, as it were, from within the individual himself and seek their fulfillment in the individual. The fact remains that even just within a framework of immanence, "secularized" subjects, while being such, nevertheless do not lose the sense of self-realization as a process of self-transcendence, that is, as the discovery, within oneself, of factors or ends greater than what each of us is able to do, and as the intuition of a free flowering and fulfillment of self, as a trace of transcendence and freedom with respect to one's own mental strategies and moral efforts, which alone would fail to achieve that fullness and happiness, but remain instead a "gift" for us mortal beings (we will return to this several times in the chapters of this book). In short, secularization does not necessarily mean losing the intuition and experience of the invisible—that is, of the ideal, of otherness, of ultimate meaning—by reducing it to the merely visible. It's just that the "roadmap" has changed: meaning no longer seems to come from outside (it would be meaning without me) but can only awaken from within, and indeed coincides with how we feel about ourselves.

But there are also those who have wanted to emphasize this possibility of a faith in the invisible (however immanent), to the point of speaking of a real phenomenon of desecularization and reenchantment of the world. Such a phenomenon, even disregarding the very different forms in which it expresses itself, would reveal how in the time of nihilism human beings continue to perceive a strange desire for the true (and strange precisely because of the dismissal of truth as a theoretical-metaphysical conception of the world). Through and beyond all deconstructions, and even in the face of the irrelevance of religious practices for public and private life, in the same "immanent frame" *the need* for meaning emerges. The discrimination here is not between believers and nonbelievers or between theists and atheists. In fact, both might share some notion of "fullness" of life, or "human flourishing," and experience it in the course of their existence. Phil Zuckerman's attempt in this regard is significant. In a successful 2014 book entitled *Living the Secular*

Life: New Answers to Old Questions, he coined the term "awe-ism" to refer to an all-secular or atheistic perception of the sacred, which emerges in the course of experiences that are particularly significant for the person who does not believe in God. Let's give examples: the sudden awe that seizes us when we immerse ourselves in the beauty of a landscape, or let ourselves be carried away by the rhythm of a song; the feeling of "floating" when we walk with our loved one; the peace and gratitude we feel in sharing unrepeatable moments with children and friends. Zuckerman intends to show that dimensions generally judged to be typical of believers actually belong to so-called atheists as well, albeit in a totally mundane or immanent version (indeed, the very label of "atheist" in his view does not do justice to those to whom it is applied, because it flattens their identity and beliefs to what they do *not* believe in). He refers here to a sense of mystery and miracle, to a disinterested morality and belief in the betterment of humanity, to the ability to be moved by the gratuitous existence of what is there, to reverence in the presence of the complexity of nature, the infinite and the unknown origin of creatures: "An aweist is someone who admits that living is wonderfully mysterious and that life is a profound experience. . . . A freethinking, secular orientation does not mean that one experiences a cold, colorless existence, devoid of aesthetic inspiration, mystical wonder, unabashed appreciation, existential joy, or a deep sense of connection with others, with nature, and with the incomprehensible. Quite the contrary. One need not have God to feel and experience awe." Paradoxically, it is precisely the "polytheism of values," which according to Max Weber characterizes the modern world, that shows that human beings are "made" to feel emotionally the presence of the world that surrounds and touches them and that vibrates in their awe. In short, people cannot give up a perspective of meaning in order to feel fulfilled, even before socially or publicly, in the intimacy and depth of their hearts. And it doesn't matter what the sense is, only that there is a sense.

Even a few years before Zuckerman's book, Hubert Dreyfus and Sean Dorrance Kelly, in their *All Things Shining: Reading the Western Classics to Find Meaning in a Secular Age*, had proposed valuing the polytheistic dimension disclosed by nihilism. And this was for a very specific purpose: to remedy the profound and paralyzing feeling of uncertainty in people's lives, caused on the one hand by the multiplication of possibilities of choice and on the other by the lack of stable points of reference. "The burden of choice is a peculiarly modern phenomenon. It proliferates in a world that no longer has any God or gods, nor even any sense of what is sacred and inviolable, to focus our understanding of what we are." According to the two authors what is nihilistic is not really the condition in which we live, which confronts us with an indefinite number of ways to give meaning to one's existence, but rather "the idea that there is no reason to prefer any answer to any other." In this case it would be a reaction to disenchantment that is exactly as one-sided as fanaticism. But between fundamentalism and relativism there would exist a "third way," which consists in seeking within the secularized world new perspectives of meaning and even "mystical" experiences comparable to those of the religious tradition: spontaneous and selfless acts of heroism; sporting performances so sublime as to seem inspired by some divine grace; the sharing of great collective events and the sense of fellowship that pervades us on such occasions. Thus, forms of life marked by self-care and self-cultivation along the lines of the Greek classics, capable of making meaning shine through the folds of an increasingly technologized and disorienting reality, are still possible. Only in this way can things shine again: "The intense and meaningful world of Homer's Greeks evidently shone with sacred force. Our technological world, by contrast, seems impoverished and dull. We cannot return to Homer's world, and we should not hope to do so. But we can become receptive to a modern pantheon of gods—to the ways in which Gehrig and Federer shine, the ways in which Marilyn Monroe or Albert Einstein changed how we see the world in which we live." Only by having a contemporary experience of the sacred can we return to savoring the sacred character of the great works of the past, which thus cease to be mere historical relics and can once again come alive and radiate their meaning precisely because we experience them in a disenchanted world.

If nihilism, among its other characteristics, is realized not only as atheism but also as polytheism, the latter in turn leads to the recognition of a true dissemination of the sacred. The world is reenchanted because human beings discover or rediscover the gods that dwell in everything. One would almost say that here we are faced with a new postmodern mythology or a secular cosmogony, in which the mystery of things, their sacredness, is manifested in their very shining in our eyes. Nor does it matter to go so far as to define or determine theoretically "what" it is that shines, for in this shining, it is not the "being" of the world that is at stake, but precisely its appearance, the manifestation on the surface of one of its secret qualities. The world is all about the perception of "qualia." There is a parallel that can perhaps help us understand the question: the conception of religion proposed in the nineteenth century by the Protestant theologian Friedrich Schleiermacher—a decisive author also because he was one of the founding fathers of modern and contemporary hermeneutics, as the science of the interpretation of theological and philosophical texts and contexts, and more generally of the universal conditions of all human understanding. Schleiermacher, in his second speech in *On Religion: Speeches to Its Cultured Despisers*, states that religion's characteristic is not to define and explain the universe in its nature (as metaphysics does) nor to perfect it through our freedom (as morality does), but is pure "intuition and feeling." Religion "wants to intuit the Universe, wants to devoutly spy on it in its own manifestations and actions, wants to be grasped and filled, in childlike passivity, by its direct influences." This is that original experience called the "feeling of dependence," namely, the consciousness of oneself as part of a divine whole. Nor is it necessary, Schleiermacher says, to start from the certainty of God's existence, because even that is secondary to our *feeling* ourselves originally dependent on the infinite—whether it exists or not.

Nihilism has most often been understood as a critique of religion and even as an antireligion, but it can also be configured as a secularized version of the religious phenomenon itself. Religion in the time of nihilism is that in which reality "vibrates" in our feeling of mystery, in our sacred awe, in the collective experience of a myth that binds and consecrates our lives.

Nihilism as Denial and Escape

Nihilism, especially in its beginnings, certainly presented itself as a doctrine, although it was a doctrine meant to "mimic" and emphasize the dark and chaotic rush of life; then it developed more and more as a standardized attitude toward life: a historical-existential condition rather than a theory about the groundlessness or "nothingness" and deceptive character of truth. If it were only a theory, it would still be too pretentious, too "metaphysical," *too little* nihilistic. This is what Nolen Gertz pointed out in his *Nihilism* (2019): being nihilist does not require "that we have a specific belief about nothingness that we could identify, but instead that we are living lives that accord with the belief that life is nothing." The nihilist can be the everyday person, even one who has no particular belief about nothingness or the "nothingness" of meaning. Therefore, according to Gertz, one must be careful to guard against three risks: confusing nihilism with *pessimism*, that is, with the idea that our existence is hopeless due to the very fact that we will die; confusing it with *cynicism*, that is, with the idea that our existence is played out entirely in terms of self-interest and domination; and finally confusing it with *apathy*, that is, the condition of those who do not take pity on reality because they judge it to be empty. These three worldviews may seem nihilistic simply because they are "dark" or "depressing," but in fact they differ from nihilism because, contrary to the latter, they are self-conscious. In contrast, "you can be with a nihilist and have no idea."

The pessimist, the cynic, and the apathetic in their own way *accept* reality, albeit through the filter of their bleak view of things. Paradoxically, they make the decision to take a step toward reality or what they consider to be reality—a reality that no longer knows how to hope, in which they have no place for sincere feelings, and which is ultimately insulting and unbearable—and act accordingly. The nihilist, on the other hand, according to Gertz, is one who may be joyful, optimistic, even "idealistic," but lives in the permanent condition of denial and even rejection of reality: "Nihilism is about evading reality rather than confronting it." Rather than a "philosophy of meaninglessness," it represents a lack of courage in taking upon oneself the responsibility for the world and meaning, even if the latter is given in the terms of absence. The nihilist lives existence passively; that is the point: he does not take charge of it; he wants to watch things and not see how they really are. Even if he lives a committed life or strives for an ideal, he does not do so by measuring himself against the real, but by creating a reality in his own image. Indeed, Gertz goes so far as to identify the close proximity of nihilism to idealism insofar as idealism is contrasted with cynicism: "As the idealist focuses more and more on how reality ought to be, the idealist becomes less and less concerned with how reality is. The utopian views of the idealist may be more compelling than the dystopian views of the cynic, but dystopian views are at least focused on this world, whereas utopian views are, by definition, focused on a world that *does not exist*. It is for this reason that to use other-worldly idealism to refute this-worldly cynicism is to engage in nihilism."

Regarding this acute identification of a curious human type such as the "nihilistic idealist," it may be mentioned incidentally that although we are not talking here about pure philosophical doctrines but about existential postures and cultural attitudes, even in philosophy the term "nihilism" has been used from the beginning in strict reference to "idealism." In 1799, Jacobi wrote in a famous letter to Fichte that the latter's rationalism led to the loss or caging in of "reality" and perfectly spilled over into nihilism. With this a theoretical equation was being formulated that the next two centuries would have ample opportunity to verify. That is, nihilism is not, as one would think, tout court irrationalism, or rather it is so only as a consequence: rather, it is born and nurtured from the most extreme of rationalisms, as German (and "Western" in general) idealism historically was. It is as if to say that the Promethean belief that human reason is the ultimate measure of all that exists or does not exist is very easily reversed into its opposite, namely, that human reason can do nothing as to knowledge of the real and the true and is thus a great power inhabited at its very core by a secret, insuperable impotence.

Now, going back to Gertz, this contemporary tendency of people to avert their gaze, to be unwilling to notice reality, to shy away from the appeal and provocation it addresses to them, has been exploited by the great tycoons of technology to erect a veritable business of escapism, to pander to and increase this "escapist" inclination: "In the era of binge-watching and handheld screens, the business of escapism—the business of keeping people staring at screens—is only getting more and more successful." This nexus between nihilism and technology, however, is precisely the point Gertz leverages to expose the game of alienation and escapism. Technology, especially technology related to artificial intelligence and universal computation, does not create new values over the old ones (i.e., it is not, as one would expect, an "active nihilism"), but actually constitutes a new form, an attractive and shiny shell, for the perpetuation of old values (i.e., it is essentially a "passive nihilism"). Specifically, following the analyses of Hannah Arendt and Michel Foucault, it can be said that in this case we are referring to the old values advocated by the Enlightenment-style science of humanity, in which individuals are reduced to statistically computable anonymous data, and politics is reduced to a cost-benefit calculation. But "if technologies are not helping to create new values but are instead operating in accordance with old values, then the nihilism created by technologies can help to reveal to us the nihilistic nature of these values." In other words, if the technological world is "the realization of the dreams of the Enlightenment," to discover that it becomes increasingly nihilistic is "to see revealed that these dreams are actually nightmares, nightmares from which we need to wake up before it's too late." The nihilistic outcomes of technology can help unmask the nihilistic sense of old values and help build new ones. And in this way, nihilism could even be a resource to challenge this new technological format of old values. It will thus be necessary to begin *"fighting nihilism with nihilism,"* that is, to take seriously Nietzsche's call to overcome the instinct for decadence in order to embrace forms of "creative" existence that destroy obsolete or passively accepted values, so that new ones emerge that are more correspondent to the needs of contemporary life: "If the nihilism generated by technological progress doesn't make us too self-destructive, then perhaps instead it will make us just destructive enough to force us to finally become creative. In other words, if nihilism doesn't kill us, it might make us stronger."

From nihilism as nightmare and destruction, back to nihilism as the creation of new values: this too is basically a verification of the ambiguous meaning and dual potential of this phenomenon. Nihilism can mean habituation or escape, evasion from reality, but also liberation by way of a new meaning with which to think about unprecedented possibilities of our being in the world. In this new perspective, it is precisely technology that can help to reveal rather than hide the human (i.e., not reducible to anonymous computation) ends of society. Of course, the question remains (which we will find often later): What allows us to move from nightmare to creative wakefulness? What wakes us up to reality and the human?

Nihilism as Abolitionism and Antihumanism

Nihilism possesses such a capacity to insinuate itself into every aspect of our culture that it is used as a tool to support the causes of discriminated-against minorities or battles related to ecological issues (neuralgic dossiers in current sociopolitical debates). Certainly, activists and theorists in civil rights movements, gender and environmental battles, to mention only a few, cannot be counted tout court among the "nihilists," if it is true that their denunciations and mobilizations attest, for example, to a willingness to resist the reduction of and discrimination against certain groups of people whose rights are unrecognized or trampled upon. In this, they testify to the irreducibility of these marginalized people's experiences, needs, and rights as worth fighting for and resisting. However, very often these militant theoretical positions arise from a radical and systematic denial of those philosophical, physical, biological, cultural, economic, and political assumptions that have determined for centuries a state of affairs to be subverted. From this point of view, nihilism is not identified simply with the radicality of the critique, and thus only as the *pars destruens* of an ideology, but as its very *pars construens*, in the sense that the positive proposition, as opposed to the critique of the negative, consists in taking "negation" as a permanent and unsurpassable practice on the theoretical and political level.

As is often the case, it is in the extreme cases that tendencies and problems become evident that in the more mediated or moderate conditions remain as undercurrents, but still present as theoretical and practical potential. In some expressions of feminist or LGBTQIA+ movements, for example, nihilism is associated with the idea that no biological, social or gendered condition is given any absolute intrinsic value in itself, in the sense that each person can and should freely determine his or her own identity, that is, what he or she has chosen to be, shaping himself or herself autonomously and creatively with respect to biological needs and social constructs. A kind of nihilistic corrosion of vetero-Western stereotypes and ideals is required to really do this. But even the process of constantly redefining oneself and the social contexts of life preserves the "nihilistic" vocation to abolitionism—in which is required the abolition not only of certain unjust or repressive conditions but, in an extreme sense, precisely the human being him- or herself as "given." Significant in this regard is the locution of "gender nihilism" employed by Aidan Rowe: "Gender nihilism designates a kind of radical agnosticism at the level of (gender) identity; a refusal of the injunction to know what one is, to objectify oneself as knowledge, and to make oneself known; a persistent 'no comment' to the police who surround and suffuse us. . . . It names a possibility latent within any particular gender position: that of disidentification, of non-identification." Here gender nihilism leads to emphasizing agnosticism; not knowing, not wanting to know, and not necessarily needing to know, again showing that the real stakes are all at the cognitive level. Liberation from power has as its high road—antimodern, anti-Enlightenment, with an echo of the Foucauldian vulgate—the liberation *of* knowledge and, more so, the liberation *from* knowledge (precisely as liberation from power). And indeed it is still stressed that "gender, sex, sexuality are conceptual instruments of this form of power." To know oneself in terms of gender and to transmit that knowledge is only a belief, that is, "a historical phenomenon and an effect of power." Consequently, "gender nihilism is the lived refutation of that belief, the demonstration that life can be lived without such knowledge, and that such a life can flourish."

Moving to a different horizon of reference, the "Black philosophy," it is possible to find another extreme exemplification of the tendency to question the human in itself as an objective given, which characterizes this vein of contemporary nihilism. Calvin Warren is among the most fervent proponents of "Black nihilism," with an emphasis that I would say is Afro-pessimistic. In his *Ontological Terror: Blackness, Nihilism, and Emancipation*, he argues that the "Black Lives Matter" movement itself rests on "metaphysical" foundations and that for this reason it paradoxically helps to perpetuate rather than prevent the nefarious effects of the ongoing "black holocaust" (the reference is to the ongoing violence suffered by black people around the world and, in the United States, to the brutal murders carried out by white law enforcement, such as that of Michael Brown or George Floyd). Black humanism, which attempts to improve the condition of black people through legal means or political claims, shares, according to Warren, the same metaphysical assumptions as antiblackness racism. The fact that slavery was abolished means nothing, because "the form of antiblackness might alter, but antiblackness itself will remain a constant."

Also adopting a Heideggerian point of view, Warren argues that Western metaphysics and Black humanism are united by the reduction of Being to entity, in an attempt to deal with entity as mere "presence" and ward off "ontological terror" in the face of Nothingness. According to Warren, the "question of Negro," and its relative oblivion, is to be interpreted in the same way as the Heideggerian *Seinsfrage*. The "Negro" is a category contrived by metaphysics to exorcise its obsession with nothingness: whites need blacks to impose their presence and "dominate" nothingness; they therefore produce a surrogate (the Black ~~Being~~) to be objectified and manipulated. The erasure of Being (and Blackness) by metaphysics (and anti-Black society) leads to writing the same term with a nihilistic sign of erasure, of Heideggerian memory. "Black being embodies metaphysical nothingness, the terror of metaphysics, in an antiblack world. . . . Metaphysics is obsessed with both blackness and nothing, and the two become synonyms for that which ruptures metaphysical organization and form." Here again the problem is cognitive: metaphysics seeks to dominate nothingness by transforming it into an object determined within our representations, that is, into a perfectly calculable entity. This very nothing's terror is projected onto the black(ness) "as a strategy of metaphysics' will to power." Postmetaphysical nihilism, according to Warren, is also lacking, for while it has deconstructed metaphysics, it has forgotten the essentiality of the Negro question. It must therefore become "black," deepening Vattimo's assumption that the end of metaphysics is unthinkable without the end of colonialism and Eurocentrism (Vattimo's text is *Nihilism and Emancipation*).

The conclusion Warren reaches is that black liberation is impossible within a humanistic, and therefore metaphysical, frame of reference. Black lives cannot "count" as human, since the human has been thought of ontically on the basis of being-White (and thus according to logics that are constitutively anti-Black), while Blackness is rather the enigma of Being or, in its metaphysical version, that Nothing-Blackness that is constantly being entified and dominated (i.e., oppressed, raped, eliminated), and thus removed as a problem. Black freedom and human emancipation, therefore, do not go hand in hand. Probably even radical outcomes such as "cancel culture," which boomed precisely in the wake of Floyd's tragic death, would not be satisfactory to Warren, since revisionism and "retroactive" iconoclasm would still move within a "humanistic" horizon: erasing the inhuman features of our culture does not reset the "racist" foundation of the conception of man on which it is based. The only way to think Blackness is then to step outside the human, not to conceive of humanity as the highest of values, but to "jump" beyond it, toward that Nothingness that still remains unthought of in our time. Here emancipatory nihilism seems to reconnect with its destructive source, that of the Russians or Nietzschean "active nihilism," with one difference: that if the overcoming of humanity (and humanism) advocated by early nihilism aspired to a condition in which *another* man or a beyond-man would arise, the most extreme forms of nihilism in our time go so far as to wish for a world simply without the human.

This antihumanism echoes in a third, extreme form of contemporary "militant" nihilism, *ecological nihilism*. Taking to extremes the emancipatory, anarchist and antihumanist undertones of the nihilist tradition, as well as embracing the most driven instances of deep ecology and ecofeminism, Australian Patricia MacCormack has come to advocate the extinction of humanity as the only answer to the environmental, social, and political crisis that characterizes our time. In *The Ahuman Manifesto*, MacCormack argues that what must be permanently abolished is "human privilege," the ultimate source of all other privilege. In addition to being catastrophic for other beings on the planet, it affects human beings themselves by generating inequality, unjust hierarchies, suffering, discrimination, and exploitation. The human being is a parasite that should be eradicated, since the essence of humanness would seem to consist of a desire for self-assertion incapable of "letting be" for any other than him- or herself. And even though post- and transhumanism seem to place themselves in the perspective of overcoming the human, they continue, according to MacCormack, to want to perpetuate it, albeit in its "cyborg" version or in "avatar" mode in the metaverse. Therefore what needs to be done is to begin practicing strict veganism, to do away with all anthropocentric descriptions of what is not human, and even to stop reproducing, attempting to care for the world while waiting for the end. The catastrophe that will lead to the demise of the Anthropocene will be the world's true jubilation. "The negative value of the end of anthropo-centrism is where the jubilance of the world begins." Like saying, "Be fruitful and annihilate yourselves."

"Zen" Nihilism

The aspiration for annihilation as the natural consequence of imperma-nence (*anicca*) is the atavistic "nihilistic" trait of Eastern religions and philosophies, such as Buddhism, which, not surprisingly, holds great fascination for the denizens of the West today. And indeed, ever since Nietzsche, Western nihilism has shared some fundamental ideas with Buddhism. Antoine Panaïoti points this out in *Nietzsche and Buddhist Philosophy*. Nietzsche himself is reported to have written in an 1883 frag-ment, "I could become the European Buddha," except to add, "though frankly I would be at the antipodes of the Indian Buddha." This kind of missed encounter between Buddhism and Nietzsche, however, not only is important for historically reconstructing the sources and motives pres-ent in the philosopher's thought but also brings out a secret vocation within all kinds of nihilism: a vocation which only superficially can be identified with a mere iconoclastic program, while feeling deeper down like a fascination for the pure negation of real being and like the temp-tation to identify in the "emptiness" the true fulfillment of the self and of things. This philosophically "high" tendency possesses so much appeal in contemporary culture perhaps because, even before it is a theoretical decision or an ascetic technique, it gives voice to the sorrowful tendency of human beings to look at the world by seeing in the foreground the evidence of the passing and ending of things, rather than that of their coming to us and the giving of their presence. This is then accompanied by the simultaneous disposition to conceive of oneself as part of an im-personal life that temporarily emerges in its performances and then falls back—as happens in a very high wave of the ocean—into the indistinct, chaotic abyss of the waters, in which the whole moves around, dissolving in itself every point of resistance, such as our defenseless "I."

These are existential and theoretical dispositions that the relation-ship between Buddhism and Nietzschean nihilism make particularly significant. Indeed, Panaïoti believes that Nietzsche and Buddha both based their philosophy on two major concepts: (1) the rejection of the myth of Being as a stable reality that lies beyond or "behind" phenomenal becoming; (2) an *ethos* that attempts to respond to the tragic and necessary nature of a constitutively impermanent world. However, while Nietzsche would propose an ethics of acceptance consisting of the absolute affirmation of life (*amor fati*), Buddhist ethics would instead aim to deny life, perceived as painful and frustrating, and to mortify desire in order to finally achieve *nirvāna*. This would result in two opposite attitudes toward one's own and one's neighbor's suffering: compassionate in the case of Buddhism, fatalistic and suspicious of any feeling of pity in the case of Nietzsche. "Amor fati is nirvāna turned inside out, the overcoming of compassion the opposite of the Buddhist cultivation of compassion." In any case, approaching this "Buddhist-Nietzschean" *ethos* requires, among other things, getting rid of the ontological "lump" represented by the Self: just as no stable being is given behind phenomena, similarly our perceptions do not gravitate around any "Self" that plays the role of "core." According to Panaïoti, on this point, Buddhism and Nietzsche's philosophy would be found in the Bundle Theory of Self proposed by Hume. As can be seen at almost every step in the reconnaissance of the forms of contemporary nihilism, and even (as in this case) in reference to traditions of thought other than European and American, a figure or doctrine that has emerged in modern thought invariably comes back to memory, proving that nihilism is hardly reducible to the postmodern; it is by no means exhausted in the critique of the "idols" of modernity—and through it backward in the critique of medieval and classical thought (being, reason, conscience, the true, the just, the good)—but develops some characteristic options of the modern philosophical tradition in a radical way.

While retaining their differences, the two "ethics" presented by Panaïoti can, in his opinion, provide a chance to face today's "challenge of nihilism," namely the challenge of living a life that has definitively divorced itself from the "fable" of the true world of which Nietzsche speaks, who in *Twilight of the Idols* states, "The true world—we have abolished. What world has remained? The apparent one perhaps? But no! With the true world we have also abolished the apparent one" (see the chapter "How the 'True World' Finally Became a Fable: The History of an Error"). Panaïoti cross-references this Nietzschean analysis with the subtractive perspective of Buddhism, looking for a suggestion to go beyond the dissolution of the real and the true in an ethics that no longer needs them in order to live in pure nihilism: "At stake, ultimately, is the formulation of a human ideal in and for a world of evanescent becoming and pure immanence. . . . The challenge of nihilism is the challenge of finding some grounding for value after the collapse of the fiction on which all values formerly relied. It is, in short, the challenge of developing an ethics entirely divorced from the *wahre weltlich* fiction of Being."

Nihilism, after declaring the impossibility of knowing the world in its truth, for what it is, and after declaring that the truth and being of the real do not stand in themselves and that the knowing being itself is nothing permanent beyond the play of its perceptions, seems almost unable to bear this weakening any longer, and must somehow deal with it by taking the way out of a new nihilistic ethics. This solution may seem strange indeed, considering that historically nihilism had arisen precisely from an assault on the sky of traditional morality, singling out Socratism and Christianity as responsible for human decadence. It would seem that the very locution "nihilist ethics" is a contradiction in terms. Yet this seems to be the prospective conclusion of the nihilist thought most ingrained in the mentality and culture of the people of our time: an ethics that takes place between acceptance of the eternal necessity of the world and compassion for the nullity of being and the self. Acceptance and compassion for nothingness. But this is to say that the decisive game of the nihilism of our time is played out in the consciousness of individuals, in the self encountering the possibility of choosing between being and nothingness, knowing that this is not a dry alternative or a dialectical opposition, but a permanent option of the reason and freedom of human beings.

In the following chapters we will encounter again, directly or indirectly, the positions I have identified in this cartography of contemporary nihilism. Indeed, the problems I will address from time to time will constitute a verification of the different perspectives presented in this report. And while it is true that each of the positions I have presented constitutes a way of solving the problems posed by nihilism, and more so of addressing the problem *that is* nihilism itself, my method will be to take these positions not only as standard theories of today's philosophical and cultural debate but as factors in a broader "critique of nihilism." This critique is in a twofold sense: a critique that nihilism has proposed of values, concepts, and attitudes affirmed only by tradition and not by free conviction, and at the same time a critique directed at nihilism itself, in order to verify whether the solutions it proposes from time to time really live up to its questions.

CHAPTER TWO

NIHILISM, ZERO POINT

To begin our journey, I would like to start from the end of a great book that, like all great books, offers us the experience of a look at ourselves and the world that we wouldn't normally have. And nevertheless when we encounter this look, it reawakens our own look and leads us to notice the real with our own eyes. It is, nevertheless, the kind of perspective that, when we encounter it, awakens in us the same look, and not because we replicate it, but because we suddenly realize that it is our own. The book is *The Road*, by Cormac McCarthy. It is the story of a loving relationship between a father and his son, as they cross—in a literal sense, before metaphorically—the devastated and desperate desert of the world in the aftermath of an unspecified nuclear catastrophe. There, where everything would seem to have burned down—from the trees and houses, to the courage to live in the soul—what resists the destruction and allows them little by little not only to go on in the instinct for survival but also to advance in desire and hope is the heart of the father and son.

Heavily burdened by a lacerating past, continuously besieged by the violence of the present, and exposed without any protection to the threat of the future, the heart reveals itself as an irreducible experience: "Because we're carrying the fire," the two protagonists say to each other. And they can say it, overcoming the nothingness that looms and is about to rob them of their "I," because they feel an inexplicable preference marking their lives—like a call to be, through the gaze and the hand of the other—and from this attachment/awareness is born in them a gratitude that allows them to fight and resist. At the very end of this journey, the two of them have escaped the ferocity of predators—humans now reduced to subhuman beings—and witnessed the sudden, radical disappearance of everything that constituted their world up until now. And in this moment, when the most dramatic detachment and at the same time the most liberating encounter occurs, McCarthy brilliantly resolves all the tension of the story of these saved lives, finding in the memory of humans—indeed in the memory of the human—the key to the future. This memory does not evoke anything from the past, but is rather like a trace of the past, I would say a fossil, that revives, that comes to life. This memory consists in listening again, in front of every circumstance, to the discreet and indestructible promise that inhabits our consciousness and our very bodies. This feeble voice—gentle and importunate at the same time—has within itself the strength to make itself heard through the dull hum of nothingness.

The life of human beings is such because it is affirmed in relation to, or in the face of, nothingness. If we did not look at nihilism—at that which is always there ready to erode the meaning of our being in the world—if we did not look at it, and go through it, without having an inkling of nihilism, we would not be human. It is through this alternative between being and nothingness that we come to understand the stature of our selves, even beyond the fact or whether this struggle sees us victorious or losing. Indeed, it is precisely when we give in to nothingness, when we consider the meaning of everything impossible, that the memory of being is reborn—through a glance, a relationship, an encounter.

Thus concludes *The Road*:

Once there were brook trout in the streams in the mountains. You could see them standing in the amber current where the white edges of their fins wimpled softly in the flow. They smelled of moss in your hand. Polished and muscular and torsional. On their backs were vermiculate patterns that were maps of the world in its becoming. Maps and mazes. Of a thing which could not be put back. Not be made right again. In the deep glens where they lived all things were older than man and they hummed of mystery.

Everything—even trout from a spring—bears a meaning inscribed within it that makes it vibrate, makes it murmur and almost whisper in telling us its being. This being must be seen, but it must also be heard, because it is never a mere classification of the world, but a story that precedes us, and which at the same time needs us to listen to it in order for it to tell itself. Every thing—every char—carries within itself the map of the world: it belongs to a whole in which only its peculiarity can be detached. And in order to understand the whole—that is, a possible sense of the world—we must be able to intercept it on the back of the fish, in the particular, sometimes hidden, folds of existence.

Looking for and deciphering the meaning of what is is always, to a greater or lesser degree, like maneuvering in a labyrinth: we can get lost in it, because the thread we are following can break. The world is never given once and for all, but it is given *in becoming*; that is, it is more or less sensibly constituted thanks to the genius of those who inhabit it. The genius of mankind lies precisely in this ability to decipher reality without wanting to and without ever being able to "put it in place," to "fix" it in our schemes. Reality cannot be readjusted, simply aligned with our intentions, because it precedes us and exceeds us. But without our gaze, it would not even exist; it would be nothing to us. Only an attentive gaze can notice the mysterious—because not taken for granted—giving of things with respect to nothing.

The following essays would like to be a shared exercise of this perspective, this way of looking: an attempt to listen to what the nihilism of our time is telling us.

CHAPTER THREE

GLIMMERS IN THE DARK

Nihilism has reemerged as a significant problem, in people's lives and in the events of the world. While its victory was almost hidden in the folds of individuals' lives, it seemed nevertheless to have won, definitively and quietly, in the societies of the advanced West, achieving a universal dominance accelerated by world globalization and an increasingly developed information technology. It is the pervasive conception that marks the most diverse worldviews, united by a tacit recognition that there is no longer a meaning to reality, an ultimate sense of oneself and of things, that can really "take hold" of our lives in the present, conquer and change us—that is, make us free.

Certainly, values remain (solidarity, legality, care for the environment . . .), as duties to which we should direct our ethical responsibility. And yet these often resonate as sadly beautiful words, incapable of overcoming that dull feeling that we are all destined to simply end. A consensual divorce seems to have been consummated between life and its meaning: life is identified with the naked desire to want itself, as an instinct of self-affirmation; and meaning is reduced to an uncertain cultural construction, made up of what we would like to be, of what we believe we are entitled to, of what the social system presents to us as an obligation.

While nihilism seemed to have won, it was a strange victory. Nihilism was no longer due to the ever-increasing "power of the spirit" (the superman as will to power). On the contrary, it was that "passive nihilism" which is rather the "decline and recession of the power of the spirit," so that, as Nietzsche writes, "previous goals and values have become incommensurate and no longer are believed; so that the synthesis of values and goals (on which every strong culture rests) dissolves and the individual values war against each other: disintegration—and whatever refreshes, heals, calms, numbs emerges into the foreground in various disguises, religious or moral, or political, or aesthetic, etc." (*Will to Power*).

This was an inverted outcome, so to speak: not the revolutionary attack against the idols of the clerical bourgeoisie—which still resounded in '68—but the educated and "correct" style of a radical mass bourgeoisie (of which Augusto Del Noce had spoken). Having now become a quiet product of consumer society, nihilism no longer meant the radical questioning of truth, but the cross-play of opinions, in which each has the right to exist, as long as it doesn't claim to be anything more than an opinion.

Now, however, a new breach seems to be opening into this narrative fabric. In the widespread "staging" of nihilistic culture, thanks also to the digital interconnection of all possible information on the face of the earth, to ask whether there is a greater meaning than this connective network (greater not in the extensive sense, but in the intensive sense—that is, the sense that has something to do with why I, just I am in the world) would be branded as the myth of the "conspiracy," to use the brilliant formula suggested in the novels of Umberto Eco. The liberation *from* sense was presented as the promise of the liberation of the ego; and instead it has led to the emptying of the person's experience. Rather than becoming the creators of their own destiny, people are instead lords of the void. This is because there is sense and destiny only when the ego recognizes (even if only to contest it!) an other, not as its own dialectical projection, but as irreducible to itself, an other whose most appropriate name may be that of "you" or "father-mother" (the generators) or "friend."

And it is exactly here that nihilism returns as a "problem," to disturb us as it did at the beginning (who remembers Dostoyevsky's *Karamazov*?), and perhaps even more radically than before. Now, in fact, this word, "nihilism," no longer indicates (only) *the phenomenon of a loss* but also (and above all) *the emergence of a need*, the making visible of a desire for meaning as a desire to "be," like the impossible flowering of a seedling from the dry and stony earth.

From this point of view, nihilism is today, paradoxically, not an obstacle, but a *chance for* the search for truth, precisely because of the anti-idolatrous force that it has deployed. At the moment when not only the old values of tradition have collapsed, but also the anthropocentric claim to replace them with the pure will of power, individuals have ultimately become irrelevant, that is, interchangeable, or purely random in the great web of the world. And it is here that something *irreducible* shows itself again in its nakedness. It is as if an "I" were asking to be born again, that is, looking for something—a glance, an encounter, a factor external to itself—that reveals to it what its being is made of, or rather that calls it to be itself.

One of the most urgent, and also most attractive, tasks for the understanding of our historical moment is precisely to intercept and follow some of the points of light where this mutation of nihilism, from a loss to the emergence of a need, is taking place. One writer who has described this shift in the most emblematic way is Michel Houellebecq. In his latest novel, *Serotonin*, we find the still open wound of this desire to be. The protagonist, Florent-Claude, literally tries to *do away with* his own self, starting with that living trace of himself that is sexual desire. In order to liquidate oneself, one must calm down; in order to calm down, one must take that blessed drug; but the action of the drug reduces precisely the libido, the last remaining sign of life. However, it is precisely the appeasement of the sexual impulse that brings to the surface what until then had been hiding behind the repetition of instinct, namely the desire to be loved and the joy of discovering that someone really loves us, even if we do not have the courage to focus our whole life on this look. The dramatic point of no return is when Florent-Claude realizes that he has lost that absolutely unique chance for himself: to accept the undeserved preference from a woman, Camille. The real is no longer able to conquer us, even if it is what we secretly most want, so reduced is our freedom, so unaccustomed are we to its taste, reducing it to pure chance or unmotivated arbitrariness.

Yet even this loss does not reset the human; and it is precisely in the protagonist's attempt at self-extinction that something seems to impose itself—almost in spite of him—that cannot be renounced: the nature of the human subject is so *objective* that he or she can never simply dispose of it as he or she pleases. It is a sort of call of the ego to itself, which comes Augustinianly from within him or her, but of which he or she cannot be the master. Toward the end he writes thus, "I had no hopes and I was fully aware that I had nothing to hope for. My analysis of the situation seemed complete and certain. There are areas of the human psyche that remain little-known because they haven't been much explored. . . . Those areas can hardly be approached except by the use of paradoxical and even absurd formulas, of which the phrase hope beyond all hope is the only one that really comes to mind. . . . I had entered an endless night, and yet there remained, deep within me, there remained something less than a hope, let's say an uncertainty."

It seems like nothing, a glimmer in the deep and seemingly endless darkness of the night. But it is also the telltale sign of a crack in nihilism; and it takes a deep sincerity with oneself not to deny it right away. Is it then *just* an uncertainty? The last page of this journey toward the loss of the self reveals that in reality a countermovement was acting under the surface, which the protagonist discovers in a final acknowledgment. Desire, hope, and uncertainty itself are real *signs* of an objective meaning embedded in our own flesh, in the very flesh of the world. And so, as if in an inverted perspective, if we have lost sense, it is the Sense itself, *in flesh and blood*, that searches for us: "God takes care of us; he thinks of us every minute, and he gives us instructions that are sometimes very precise. Those surges of love that flow into our chests and take our breath away—those illuminations, those ecstasies, inexplicable if we consider our biological nature, our status as simple primates—are extremely clear signs."

Clear, that is, to the point of giving a name to this gaze, to the point of identifying the loving subject who, in his carnality, reawakens desire: "And today I understand Christ's point of view and his repeated horror at the hardening of people's hearts: all of these things are signs, and they don't realise it." Taking the *signs into account*: perhaps this is the simple way that is given to us to go through nihilism. Indeed, to recognize this path, with poverty of spirit, is already the first indication that we have in some way begun to overcome it.

CHAPTER FOUR

INTELLIGENCE IS
NOT AUTOPILOT

Given the shift in the meaning of nihilism that we have just explored, the challenge is this: in order to understand the historical moment we are living in, marked by the long shadow of nihilism, we need to intercept those points of light in which the emptiness of meaning that until now appeared only as a loss of values and ideals slowly—but inevitably—changes into the emergence of a need. Only then can we verify if there is something irreducible that "resists" the great reduction.

Among the factors that deserve prominent consideration in this regard is the nature of our own "intelligence," a faculty so taken for granted that it has become foreign to us. What does it mean to be intelligent people? The question seems idle, so 'natural' is the exercise of this faculty for our being in the world. And yet it is not. Almost without realizing it, we have increasingly identified our intelligence as a sort of "autopilot," a function of calculation of complex data, which tries to find for each problem the simplest solution, schematizable in a procedure. That this is a special capacity, and also an exciting performance of our intelligence, is certainly true. But if it is detached from, or considered independent of, our broader capacity to ask for meaning about us and about things, it becomes only an "'artificial' intelligence." But it is precisely artificial intelligence, dominating the layers of our time and lives through its algorithms (for which we can only be grateful given the incredible facilitation it offers us in living), that once again poses to us the question of what intelligence is for a human being. It is so easy to skip the question, considering the computational capacity not only as an effect of our intelligent openness to the world, but even more as its original nature. This is so true that we are increasingly tempted to assume artificial intelligence as the criterion of measurement to know and verify our—let's call it "natural"—intelligence.

Here we find one of the typical characteristics of contemporary nihilism, in which the emptiness of meaning is conveyed—and most often hidden—by the technical organization of the world, and in which the search for the meaning of existence is surrogated in the increasingly controlled calculation of its possibilities and problems. Paradoxically, the more that strategies for solving the various problems inherent in the organization of our personal and social life increase (fortunately!), the more dramatically the problem that is life itself—that is, the question about the meaning of reality—becomes blurred. With this I do not want to say—as one is tempted to do by taking "romantic" shortcuts—that the lack of an ultimate meaning for life depends on the progress of our calculating intelligence: on the contrary, these very advances force us to ask ourselves what is the root from which they spring, because we can only calculate what we recognize as a datum that challenges us and that to some extent we manage to "love."

All the less convincing is the opposition between a "calculating" thought and a "meditating" thought: a lexicon suggested by Heidegger, but which is most often misunderstood precisely because it is considered as an alternative. Let's think, for example, about how a Heideggerian such as Hubert Dreyfus, starting from *Dasein* as being-in-the-world, has shown that human intelligence is not reducible only to its computational skills—as cognitivism and, in particular, research programs on artificial intelligence would like—but is able to perform operations that escape the formalizations of computer languages. Our mind, in other words, would possess specific structures and operations of an unconscious, historical, cultural, and existential kind, in a broad sense not reproducible according to the schemes of digital procedures (we will come back to this in chapter 18).

But rather than stopping at the simple and in many ways obvious distinction between what would be irreducible in a specifically human or "natural" intelligence and what would instead be replicable or programmable with computer supports, we must pose the problem of the possible implications. In fact, we can ask ourselves if the subject that calculates can continue to do so without bringing into his own calculation the imprint of his interrogative intelligence, with the consequence of becoming himself—the subject—the most iron "object" of calculation. To understand what this is really about, we need only ask a simple question, always implicit in our daily experience: in all our actions, in all our relationships with things and people, we move only if *we understand that something is there for us in the world*. Isn't it true that our experience as conscious and free persons is increased when we discover that reality—faces, objects, encounters, events—comes to meet us and touches us, provokes us, asks something of us, waits for our response?

Noticing reality: this is the burning point on which our being in the world depends. Everything is played out in the way we perceive being— that is, *what we are*, what things are, and all the more radically if we do not take for granted *the very fact* that we are there and that reality exists. This is not an abstract reflection, but the most concrete, most "carnal" factor of our existence, because it is the one in which our "I" is most at stake in its relationship with the daily data of experience. But as often happens in experience, it is in the moment of crisis that we feel, paradoxically, the need left by what does not work, or what we lack. Thus, it is precisely the increasing reduction of this knowledge of reality in our time that forces us to understand how essential it is for the realization of our person.

When I speak of knowledge reduction, I certainly do not mean the amount of information we are able to collect and manage, even if only virtually. From this point of view, the development of our knowledge is now potentially indefinite, insofar as everything *we would like to* know is available to us. But, precisely, what do we want to know? From what does our interest arise? What or who moves our desire and our curiosity? This is the truly critical point of contemporary society and culture, in which we are witnessing a quantity of "knowledge" that often risks keeping us from really "knowing" anything, because the subject of knowledge itself risks being missed. Or rather, the subject tends to be replaced by what certain cultural, commercial, and political interests induce it to want. This is the currently much debated problem of *Big Data*, the hypertrophic extension both of universal knowledge and of the particular preferences of each single user in the great network of knowledge: preferences that those who manage computer networks can accumulate, orient, and control thanks to the detection (moreover illegal) of individual choices, drawn from the most shared social media, such as Facebook, Twitter, or Instagram. In such a context, how do we perceive the world? On what basis do we perceive as "true" what we have known? As Danah Boyd (an American researcher dedicated to the study of media literacy) has written, quoting Cory Doctorow, "We're not living through a crisis about what is true, we're living through a crisis about how we know whether something is true. We're not disagreeing about facts, we're disagreeing about epistemology"—that is, the way in which our knowledge is formed. If in fact we do not have a reasonable certainty—or at least sufficient confidence—that what we perceive is true, we will be doomed to never come into contact with the real.

But there is also the inverse: if we do not come to critically evaluate whether everything we perceive is true (or if it is sometimes not true), or even if something we do not immediately perceive happens to be true, then we will inevitably be condemned to confuse reality with our subjective perceptions. This was effectively brought into focus by an article by Sabino Cassese in the magazine *7* ("La cattiva politica schiava della percezione" [The bad policy enslaved by perception], *Corriere della sera*, September 13, 2018). But already the same newspaper had anticipated on August 31 a survey by the polling company IPSOS in which it appeared that Italy and the United States are among the countries in which the tendency to perceptual distortions of reality is most widespread (for example, on economic growth, migration flows, the health care system, and the number of murders), and also those in which, in politics, "the most profound change in the relationship between voters and elected officials" has occurred. Complicating the issue is the ever-increasing conditioning of the digital environment in which we are continuously immersed (just think of our dependence on smartphones and the internet), and which acts not only on the "construction" and selection of news but also on the very conformation of our mental and perceptive processes to this information. So much so that the truth of a piece of information, and consequently the reliability of a piece of knowledge, can be real or simply *made-up*, constructed as fake news, in some cases even only through graphic design or a certain perceptual strategy that—thanks to a mechanism of visual attraction—blocks the attention on news headlines, which can then turn out to be ambiguous or deviant.

Katy Steinmetz, among many analysts, discussed this in an article in *Time* magazine in August 2018 on the subject of *fake news*, according to which "Robots and propagandists are only part of the problem. The bigger issue is your brain." The "illusory truths" depend on the fact that "we make quick decisions about what's reliable *online*" based on habit and the repetitiveness of the messages we get online: "The higher something appears in Google search results, the more reliable it is. But Google's algorithms are surfacing content based on keywords, not truth. If you ask about using apricot seeds to cure cancer, the tool will dutifully find pages asserting that they work."

The issue is so widespread and slippery (also for the use that economic and political forces make of it) that it has been called "the equivalent of a public health crisis." Someone thinks that the falsifications of truth and reality caused (indirectly) by the algorithms can be remedied by putting in place other algorithms that identify the *accounts* or Facebook pages from which the false news starts and spreads, in order to block them. But this countermeasure will never be enough, because at stake is the mental and moral process by which we give and receive trust in communicating with each other. Only a "human factor" can re-open the game; only a path of education can make us "stop and think" what we instinctively or mechanically would be inclined to accept and share as "true," but which perhaps is not. As the *Time* article concludes, "Teachers must . . . train students to be skeptical without making them cynical," that is, to critically test their belief in reality.

As I said, every crisis puts us at a crossroads. We could give in to fear and slip into pessimism, believing that by now we are all inevitably "played" by the great machine of digital communication and that at the very moment when we seem to have the maximum of possible tools to know and manipulate the world, we are actually deprived of the very freedom to be ourselves and not what the system of algorithms has decided to make of us. But we could also—more reasonably—ask ourselves if there is something in our experience that *we care to* save, something about us that we would not easily give up, something in reality that seems too precious to be denied. In this way, perhaps this cognitive crisis can be the opportunity we are given to regain a path of knowledge, not only automatically acquired, but critically verified. And the verification consists in discovering whether or not knowing reality increases the subject of knowledge: not so much (or not only) because it makes him more powerful or performant in his strategies, but because it reawakens in him the question about the "meaning" of himself and of the world, about the connection between things and between things and himself. This turning point, however, cannot arise from a mere epistemological theory; on the contrary, the stakes and the method of knowledge can and must be discovered by each of us, starting from those moments or instances in our conscious life in which we have experienced a knowledge that has mobilized and changed our self. This means, however, that the very idea of reason or intelligence, usually understood as the ability to analyze, calculate, and predict the effects of our actions, needs to be broadened and made more of a "lived" understanding of reason. Rationality is not a cold procedure, but is the way in which we—in the totality of our dimensions—live in reality.

Therefore, at the very problematic crossroads between artificial intelligence and natural intelligence, we must no longer take for granted the way in which an intelligent being experiences reality as such. There is a text by the great thinker Simone Weil (dating back to the forties and included in the collection *Waiting for God*) that helps us to understand the full extent of intelligence, showing that it embodies the mystery of the human being. Intelligence, says Weil, referring in particular to the activity of study on the part of young people (but it applies to all moments in which we are truly interested in something) consists above all in "paying attention." It is something simple and apparently minimal, but it is the key to our being in the world, the moment in which our self can discover the unimaginable presence of things. And not by an effort of will, but by the allure of an attraction.

This is Weil's description: "The intelligence can only be led by desire. For there to be desire, there must be pleasure and joy in the work. The intelligence only grows and bears fruit in joy." Attention is like the exercise of desire on the part of the intelligence, which discovers its willingness to let itself be touched by the real: "We have to press on and loosen up alternately, just as we breathe in and out." Attention "consists of suspending our thought, leaving it detached, empty, and ready to be penetrated by the object." However, it is not at all "natural" in the sense of obvious or taken for granted: on the contrary, Weil continues, "something in our soul has a far more violent repugnance for true attention than the flesh has for bodily fatigue. This something is much more closely connected with evil than is the flesh. That is why every time that we really concentrate our attention, we destroy the evil in ourselves."

Could it be that today nihilism is concentrated precisely in this strange tendency of ours to inhibit our desire and to detach ourselves from the beauty and joy of discovery? It is at this level that the game is essentially played out: to regain possession of our intelligence in its entirety, without giving in to the fear of losing ourselves and our security with respect to the unexpectedness of reality. Our "evil," as we have read, is in fact not primarily due to a lack of moral behavior, but to a defect of intelligence in the face of the incalculable call of being.

CHAPTER FIVE

THAT GAP BETWEEN KNOWLEDGE AND AFFECTION

In order to know things, I observed earlier, we need to love them. A look of affection is required even when we use our intelligence as a mere calculating procedure. This affective dimension should not be understood, however, as a "sentimental" addition or as a subjective emotion in contrast to the cold observation of the objective data of reality. On the contrary, this affection constitutes the underlying motivation in all our cognitive acts, an opening of our mind that seeks the meaning of things. We can describe it as an "attraction" that reality—things, people, nature, events—always exerts on our ego, calling it and challenging it to a journey of discovery. But the question is not automatic, because it has to do with our freedom: the critical point is whether we accept or decline this invitation of reality, and therefore whether we support or mortify this original affection for being.

One of the most disturbing and dramatic signs of the nihilism of our age is that of having progressively detached the cognitive moment from the affective moment of our experience in such a way that it becomes possible, indeed almost necessary, to divest ourselves of the question of the ultimate meaning of things in order to know them objectively. A strange situation has been created. The nihilism of the twentieth century was born as a violent reaction to the claims of the positivism of the late nineteenth century, for which reality is made only of empirical data quantitatively measurable and manageable by science. The more the latter progressed in its explanations of the world, the more the world lost that sense of metaphysical or religious "mystery" that was declared the mere product of ignorance. Now, however, it seems that "meaning," the ancient adversary of nihilism (in front of which Nietzsche could proudly proclaim that "there are no facts, but only interpretations"), paradoxically finds its full revenge in the phase of contemporary *technological* nihilism, which recognizes that even the techno-scientific knowledge of the world engages in a process of the "construction" of reality, in which measurement and calculation are not limited to "real" data, but determine them and somehow "create" and reproduce them. Nietzschean "interpretations" have become the digital productions of the world.

But without personal meaning it is not possible to live, as our daily experience attests. Without meaning, life would be unbearable. Here, then, lies the safety device that is introduced to solve the problem: meaning must be moved from the field of knowledge to that of feeling. The meaning, if there is one, must be found in our emotions. It is no longer a question of reality, but of "feeling." Meaning no longer belongs to ontology, but to psychology; it no longer has anything to do with the recognition of the truth of existence, but with the cultural construction of one's own "self," with a "self-poiesis," to put it in the lexicon of cultural anthropology (I am thinking of an author such as Francesco Remotti). After all, love in the time of nihilism is a form of widespread sentimentalism (like the reverse side of the coin of a purely technical intelligence): it is what we feel, moved by the emotional states that always determine our mood, but that, if they become a closed horizon, do not refer to anything else outside of our reaction. The real problem of reducing love to a mere feeling is that in this way, we reduce the feeling itself, precisely because we separate it from the judgment of reason, blocking it as a purely subjective factor. And in turn this reduces the subject to the action/reaction mechanism of instinct.

But as is often the case in forced fragmentations, in each of the pieces the trace of the relationship with the other remains. And if it is true that, in order to be fully itself, knowledge needs an affective openness to being, so too, to be fully itself, affection requires a judgment of knowledge: this is what makes love vibrate in all its chords. The experience of an attraction that moves us then becomes the track to experience on one's own skin, or in one's own bowels (according to a biblical expression taken up by the philosopher María Zambrano), the ultimate meaning of reality. It is a sense that is experienced, suffered, loved, or missed—and for this truly understood. A sense that can be understood precisely because it expands one's individual feeling to the entire cosmos.

A writer like David Foster Wallace understood this with great sensitivity, and many have seen him as the emblem of a painful and ironic description of the difficulty, if not the impossibility, of affirming an ultimate sense of self. Instead, it seems he constitutes one of the most poignant testimonies to the fact that without this possibility, one cannot live, and that life is indeed this very "possibility" of a meaning greater than oneself. In one of his most famous texts, "This Is Water," a speech he gave in 2005 at Kenyon College's graduation ceremony, Wallace talks about this very possibility. And he does it through a memorable example: a guy comes home tired and stressed from work, but he remembers that he has nothing in the fridge, and so he is forced to head for the chaotic hell of a supermarket to do his shopping. Only there he meets all the other guys who have the same unbearable "destiny": to undergo the stress of beastly traffic, the confusion, the deafening music, the endless queues at the few open tills: "But anyway, you finally get to the checkout line's front, and you pay for your food, and wait to get your check or card authenticated by a machine, and you get told to 'Have a nice day' in a voice that is the absolute voice of death." Then return to your car to drive home, again going through tremendous traffic filled with SUVs, Hummers, and V12 trucks. Inside this situation, however, as inside every other situation, there is always a basic choice of action, whether conscious or unconscious; a posture of the ego and a perspective of one's gaze in which from the beginning we have already decided what to see and how to see it. But the fact is that we can *choose* this posture, we can decide to take on that perspective or not. And everything else depends on this: for example, "if I don't make a conscious decision about how to think and what to pay attention to, I'm gonna be pissed and miserable every time I have to food shop."

As a matter of fact, we are usually no longer even faced with a choice on how to relate to reality, because a way of thinking that is so obvious and reactive—Wallace calls it "my basic configuration"—is triggered in such a way that we no longer notice what surrounds us and what happens to us. I just know (and have known all along) that all the other patrons of the supermarket—except me, of course—are there to annoy me, to get in my way. And that seems "deeply unfair" to me. Just look at them: "How repulsive most of them are and how stupid and cow-like and dead-eyed and nonhuman they seem here in the checkout line . . . talking loudly on cell phones in the middle of the line." And yet we could also look at them through the filter of our correct socio-humanistic and ecological beliefs. Then we would think how our children and grandchildren may condemn us for wasting natural resources intended for them, out of purely selfish and consumerist reasons.

The writer describes this situation of absolute, anonymous normality as the merciless mirror of anthropocentrism and of the most driven egocentrism, that is, "the automatic, unconscious belief that I am the center of the world and that my immediate needs and feelings are what should determine the world's priorities." But in all this we always have the possibility—and therefore the freedom—to look at the world from another point of view, with another consciousness, open to an affective judgment—that is, to recognize that in the world there is something worthy of being loved and that there is a meaning greater than my automatic schemes. Thus I might choose to see in another, more acute and poignant way the people I am looking at. Perhaps they are not annoying obstacles to the comfortable achievement of my purposes, but persons whose lives are harder and more problematic than mine. For example, I might "choose to look differently at this fat, dead-eyed, over-made-up lady who just screamed at her kid in the checkout line . . . ; maybe she's been up three straight nights holding the hand of her husband, who's dying of bone cancer . . ." In short, there is always another way of looking at the world, and this unprecedented possibility, offered to our free choice, is the possibility of *loving* the world: "It will actually be within your power to experience a crowded, hot, slow, consumer-hell-type situation as not only meaningful, but sacred, on fire with the same force that lit the stars—compassion, love, the subsurface unity of all things." And then, as a man of our time, Foster Wallace adds, "Not that that mystical stuff's necessarily true . . ." meaning it's not about imagining another world outside of reality, to sublimate the pain and discomfort of living. Rather, "The only thing that's capital-T True is that you get to decide how you're going to try to see it."

Here is the question to be left open: On what basis can we decide how to look at the world? All the risk of accepting or refusing the invitation is left to our freedom: of seeing, and of wanting the good of ourselves and of everything. But we can want this good only because on some occasion—in some face, in some event—it has wanted us. In the "daily boredom" and in the "senselessness" we experience, where nothingness is always waiting for us, even in the queue of the checkout line at a supermarket, this other way of looking can return to us, and turn on "the Love that moves the sun and the other stars" (Dante, *Paradise* 33).

CHAPTER SIX

THE INFINITY WITHIN

There is a great paradox that accompanies the history of nihilism from the beginning and that today we see more clearly in its fulfillment: the true meaning of the "death of God"—the formula that, since Nietzsche, alludes to the irreversible crisis of all transcendence, ontological, religious or moral—lies in the death of the "I." The being that I am is no longer to be thought of as an objective "given," but as the subjective "case" of an impersonal evolutionary process, a moment of temporary transit: what Eastern nihilism, inspired by Buddhism, would call the "nonpermanence" (*anicca*) or the "nonexistence" (*anattā*) of the individual self. Accidental moments in the necessary flow of nature: that's what human beings would be; and it's by no means certain that the lack of personal meaning is a loss. According to some, it might even be a liberation, the possibility to live life for what it is, in its naked happening—and that's it.

This paradox is the serious situation of today's culture. On the one hand, in fact, the ideology of performance seems to impose itself on all fronts, whereby our being consists in succeeding—reducing success, however, to the affirmation of our own image of power (whatever that may be). On the other hand, if this game does not "succeed"—and often it does not succeed, or succeeds badly, or simply does not last—our being is literally annihilated, becomes nothing, and is no longer of any use. This is where that "culture of waste" is born, in which Pope Francis clearly identifies one of the most dramatic problems of our society.

But what can question this perspective—not only a socioeconomic one, but first of all an anthropological one—of the "discarding of the self"? The appeal to an individual wisdom or to a public morality is no longer effective: deontology is not able to come to grips with ontology. Will there ever be a point at which we can raise the issue? But if there is, it cannot come from outside experience, but can only arise from within it. A point gained from the very urgency of living that troubles us every day; a point that emerges from the very immanence of life. If a transcendent meaning exists, either it must be traced in immanence or it simply does not give itself.

Here the existential problem of nihilism is rekindled. It is rekindled where life seems to be an "absolute immanence," to use the expression of the philosopher Gilles Deleuze (in *L'immanence: Une vie...* of 1995 [*Pure Immanence*]), which takes up a typical idea of Spinoza, according to which life is absolute natural power, "a movement that never begins nor ends," impersonal consciousness, at the same time "with neither object nor self" (however strange a consciousness that is not consciousness of "something" and that is not a consciousness of itself may be to common sense). Only a "pure immanence," according to Deleuze, would allow a "complete bliss": like that of "very small children" that "all resemble one another and have hardly any individuality, but they have singularities: a smile, a gesture, a funny face—not subjective qualities. Small children, through all their sufferings and weakness, are infused with an immanent life that is pure power and even bliss." In short, we could say that when the single newborn becomes an "individual" or "self," when it acquires a personal irreducibility, then life is lost. And an illusory transcendence would impose itself, with the intention of signifying life in relation to something or someone greater than life, which in reality betrays and sclerotizes it. Deleuzian life is a movement without origin and without purpose, a power that feeds itself, a desire that continues to produce itself without feeling any lack. The only possible meaning, then, is the one that is not imposed, but produced by the events of lives themselves, which find only in themselves and never in something other than themselves their random direction.

I found the echo of this thesis in the observation of one of my philosophy students, who wrote to me: "I think that the value of nihilism lies precisely in the total loss of meaning, which if at first it can undoubt-edly disorient us, later it can only make us appreciate life for what it is, make us love it and make us live it to the full, trying to get the best pos-sible experience out of it." In this lies "the deepest desire to live life in its wonderful superficiality." The superficiality of life and reality is wonder-ful, for my student, precisely because it does not need anything else to be enjoyed, other than being what it is. But a simple question arises, *from within* this enjoyment: "Who" is he or she who can enjoy this wonder? To "whom" does the experience of the bliss of life happen? If everything is reduced to an impersonal power that produces itself, with nothing else and no one else missing, is there not a need for an "I," that is, one who waits, who desires, who asks, in order to enjoy—that is, in order to be happy? We are never completely happy, and yet we desire to be, precisely because all that we can have or even imagine is not enough. At the heart of our immanence there is produced—like a backlash or a countermovement—an infinity, which does not come from outside, but impinges on us from within. Without this abysmal intensity—the fact that nothing is ever enough for us—every superficiality would give us, as Leopardi wrote, only "anxiousness" and "boredom" ("Canto notturno"). We need infinity in order to enjoy finite things.

That this infinity is the most radical point of irreducibility of the life of the "I" was seen with unexpected pertinence (and for this reason is all the more convincing) by Descartes. The "I" of which Descartes speaks—the *cogito* that gives foundation to all modern thought—can well be understood as a moment of absolute immanence, if it is true that the thinking substance does not need anything else, not even its own body, to grasp itself with full evidence. A self that one might call "solipsistic." So much so that when this "I" begins to analyze the ideas present in his mind, he discovers that he could have invented them all (and therefore all his ideas could also be deceptive or illusory), except one idea, innate in us, and that is the idea of infinity. Since I am a finite substance—says Descartes—I myself cannot be the cause of this idea," and from this "it necessarily follows that I am not alone in the world." Nor is the objection valid that the idea of "infinity" would actually be constructed by our-selves, starting from the idea of a finite being, and simply denying its fi-nite characters (just as the idea of "rest" would be the negation of that of "motion" and the idea of "darkness" the negation of that of "light"). Descartes affirms instead that the question is exactly the opposite of what is thought: "The perception of the infinite in me must be in some way prior to that of the finite: the perception of God, in other words, prior to that of myself. For how could I possibly understand that I doubt, and that I desire, that is, that there is something lacking in me, and that I am not completely perfect, if there were no idea in me of a more perfect being, by comparison with which I could recognize my own shortcomings?" This is the paradox that lies at the heart of the modern subject, that subject which we would think autonomous and self-referential, centered only on itself. On the contrary, the "I" discovers in itself an Other; and without the relationship with this Other that makes it so, the "I" simply would not exist. He is not "alone" in the world: the infinite is like a *partnership*, a companionship that lies at the origin of his very being, and on which the whole activity of his intelligence and rationality also depends.

But is it not contradictory or simply impossible to think of an infinite—an infinite reality—that precedes me and with which I stand in relation? Such a relationship is only conceivable between two finites. Yes, this is true, if we understand infinity as that which is "before" and "after," or "above" or "in front of" us. In that case, what would infinity be? It would be a reality that is "produced" now, and is manifested precisely in the idea of a thinking being, who attests with his thought to what is more than thought. As Emmanuel Lévinas wrote in *Totality and Infinity* (1961), precisely about this idea in Descartes, "To think the infinite, the transcendent, the Stranger, is hence not to think an object. But to think what does not have the lineaments of an object is in reality to do more or better than think."

CHAPTER SEVEN

THE VOCATION
OF THE FLESH

With the progression of nihilism—which exploded first as a revolutionary "pathology," and finally came to be accepted as the normal condition of contemporary human life—the concept of the human being as a "spiritual" being radically changes. Already in Nietzsche's *Thus Spoke Zarathustra*, the will of the superman coincided with "remaining faithful to the earth"—installed in the biological dimension of the body—while spiritual values ended up being unmasked as mere "extraterrestrial hopes." And those who still speak of a spiritual reality in man are none other than the "mixers of poison," "despisers of life, dying off and poisoned themselves." The "spirit" belongs to an other world than the terrestrial one, an illusory and lying superworld, which covers and sublimates the telluric (and unconscious) drives that move our body. Here we glimpse another great presence, often camouflaged, effecting the philosophy of our time: Arthur Schopenhauer. His is the idea that at the bottom of reality, and in the depths of human life, there is a blind, dominating force; a will that has no purpose and no sense, if not its own will. We participate in this force through the instincts of our body and try throughout life to contain and sublimate it, but in the end, we remain powerless victims, because it is a will without reason, which ends up devouring the very subject of the will. So instinct, from being an invitation to pleasure, ends up becoming the condemnation to the most acute pain that we can experience, the thing that makes us suffer in an absurd way, without reason.

On the one hand, then, we have the ideal or the spiritual as an ultramundane heaven increasingly detached from the earth; on the other hand, the corporeal and material, as the world of the will, increasingly identified with instinct. The fact is that the spirit and the body stand together or fall together. And if we lose one, we soon lose the other. But this for Schopenhauer (and for his heirs, direct or indirect) means that what is rational, sensible, goal oriented, is actually only a transient form of the deformed, a mask of chaos. We "are" our body because the body coincides with the will, and the will is the "in itself" of the world: "The will is the innermost, the kernel of every individual thing and likewise of the whole: it appears in every blind operation of a force of nature: it also appears in deliberative human action; these differ from each other only in the grade of their appearing, not in the essence of what appears." And when Freud discovered, within his psychoanalytic practice, the power— both physiological and pathological—of the unconscious, he spoke of it as "removed" vital drives ("the repressed is the prototype of the unconscious for us," he wrote in *The Ego and the Id* of 1923), "something between flight and condemnation." But the ego can never escape from itself and its impulses: it can only condemn them through the judgment of a "Super-Ego" that inhibits the satisfaction of vital desires. Our body is inhabited and even "lived" passively—below the consciousness—by an impersonal force, which the German language refers to with the neutral pronoun "Es," according to the idea of the psychoanalyst Georg Groddeck, later adopted by Freud: "I hold the view that man is animated by the Unknown, that there is within him an "Es," an "It," some wondrous force which directs both what he himself does and what happens to him. The affirmation "I live" is only conditionally correct; it expresses only a small and superficial part of the fundamental principle, "Man is lived by the It" (Groddeck, *Book of the It*, 1923). Everything in life depends on the "It": it decides to get sick or to be healthy. It is an occult and all-pervasive power that can turn into a healthy cell as well as a cancerous cell but, by virtue of its vitality, can also become perception, thought, and will. It is unconscious and consciousness together. And yet, Groddeck concludes, "about the It itself we know nothing whatever."

It is significant that in the changed conditions of contemporary ni-hilism this impersonal force that, so to speak, acts from within the life of human beings—of "bodies" as well as of "spirits"—has been reinter-preted as a political device. A whole current of analysis of modern so-cieties, which began with Michel Foucault and proceeds up to Giorgio Agamben, has called the channeling of this force "biopolitics," identify-ing it as the great device that every "power" as such—political, economic, ecclesiastical—exercises over the lives of human beings through the nor-malization or medicalization or sterilization of the "bios." This "biopoli-tics" comes from the outside to inform and shape the inside of the life and death of human bodies, attacking the only resource of defenseless and ex-posed people, starting with their sexuality. It is precisely the human body that is increasingly considered as the real stake in solving the problem of the spiritual and, thus, comes the most under attack and control.

According to these authors, the interest of those who really rule in today's world, namely capitalist power in its extreme economic-financial form, is to defuse the naked power of bodies. This would be a trajec-tory that goes from the early modern era, with the control that priests maintained over bodies through the instrument of the "confession" of souls, to the rejection of the bodies of migrants—drifting beings dispos-sessed of their human identity—and not least to the management of the COVID-19 emergency as an opportunity to make permanent a "state of exception" typical of totalitarian regimes, the one theorized by Carl Schmitt referring to the possibility that in a given circumstance of social, political and economic crisis the sovereign power decides the suspen-sion of the ordinary laws of a state: "Along with the emergence of bio-politics, we can observe a displacement and gradual expansion beyond the limits of the decision on bare life, in the state of exception, in which sovereignty consisted." Indeed, in the ancient regime, again according to Agamben's reconstruction, the "natural life" of human beings was under-stood essentially as "creatural life," that is, directly dependent on God and therefore not directly at the disposal of political power. Moreover, even in classical ages, natural life itself, denoted by the Greek term *zōē*, was distinct from specifically political life (i.e., actualized fully in the polis), rendered by the term *bios*. Having lost the creaturely relationship and the difference between natural life and political life, a bare, naked "life" in the contemporary world "fully enters into the structure of the state"; indeed it becomes "the earthly foundation" of state legitimacy and sovereignty. The consequence is that "in modern biopolitics, sovereign is he who decides on the value or the nonvalue of life as such" (Agamben, *Omnibus Homo Sacer*).

But what can really save the body of humans, their biological life itself, *which is already* social, political? During the rise of nihilism it was believed that for this purpose it was necessary (and sufficient) to detach the corporeal from the spiritual—understood as an abstract superstructure or moral duty to be—because it was blamed for the mortification of the body. Thus the countermove was elaborated: to reduce the spiritual to the "cultural" elaboration of the corporeal, to the construction of anthropological, social and ethical-political devices. The repression of instinct made way for the liberation of instinct (and for the enormous success of the consumer society). However, as in a fatal circle, the more the body was freed, the more it was handed over helplessly to the control of the techno-efficient values of the dominant culture, and therefore to a larval form of the "spirit." And yet each of us "knows" from experience what our body is. This knowledge is acquired not only through the repetition of instinct as a mechanism of action/reaction but due to the fact that we all perceive our body as a kind of "call." The thing that struck me most during a recent surgery I underwent, going through a period when my body was not at my disposal (indeed it was jammed with many impediments and exposed to the techniques of various treatments), was that through my body I was beginning to actually understand the embodied dimension of my "spirit." My body was not just a series of tissues or nervous and blood systems; it was a body that received itself, that sought itself, that pined or cried out, that transcended its mere "soma." My body was revealing itself as a "flesh."

The flesh is our deepest—I dare say—spiritual vocation: it is our own body, the lived body (of which phenomenology has given us memorable descriptions, from Husserl to Merleau-Ponty to Michel Henry). It is a call to be ourselves—ourselves, not others—and at the same time our calling the world to us, our ability to sensitively perceive the more-than-sensible sense of life. Francis Bacon, the painter, captures this remarkably. In his work, human flesh itself becomes a cry of meaning, even to the point of being a spasm (think of one of his crucifixions in the form of a quartered animal). Bacon once said: "It is an instinct, an intuition, that pushes me to paint the flesh of man as if it were spreading outside the body, as if it were its own shadow" (Maubert, *L'odeur du sang humain ne me quitte pas des yeux: Conversation avec Francis Maubert*, dating back to the 1980s). This language is reminiscent—however high the risk—of the angel's announcement to that young woman named Mary: "The Holy Spirit will come upon you, and the power of the Most High will overshadow you" (Luke 1:35 NRSV). In fact, it is amazing to see Bacon's exposed and screaming flesh against the perfect composure of Raphael's "incarnations." Once we have seen them together, it is as if we could no longer detach them from each other, because in the divine "politeness" of Raphael's form vibrates the same shadow that divinely disquiets and deconstructs Bacon's form. The same "shadow"—that which makes the body a flesh and that makes the flesh the suffering perception of the spirit—is that in which pain and glory become friends again.

That is why I was impressed by what Julián Carrón recently wrote in a book with a strange title, as attractive as a promise (*The Radiance in Your Eyes: What Saves Us from Nothingness?*): "What can defeat the nihilism in us? Only being magnetized by a presence, by flesh that brings with itself, in itself, something that corresponds to all our expectancy, all our desire, all our need for meaning and affection, for fullness and for esteem. We will be saved from nothingness only by that flesh able to fill the 'abyss of life,' the 'mad desire' for fulfillment in us." Nihilism is like a progressive forgetting that the Word has become flesh. Perhaps then only from the flesh will it be possible to relearn—by perceiving it—this logos.

CHAPTER EIGHT

THE GRATITUDE
OF BEING BORN

The anguish that marked us in the days of the COVID-19 pandemic brought to the surface, in all the evidence, the nihilistic plot that marks from top to bottom our way of conceiving ourselves and reality. But on the other hand it has suddenly shown, with equal evidence, that nihilism is perhaps no longer up to the crisis we are experiencing in our time. It is precisely the questions that arise from the distressing health emergency that show the nihilistic structure of life and culture, of politics and society, imploding from within. The circle is broken and questions are reborn. And this is the cultural turning point: they are not reborn by force of analysis. Indeed, it is true that many times the *surplus of* analysis paradoxically risks silencing the most important questions and missing the decisive point of the situation. Because the point is ourselves, and the questions are reborn as the "form" of our being in the world.

The impression is that something is giving way, and we find ourselves unable to sustain the impact of an unpredictable reality with our usual categories: a pathogenic virus that does not let itself be grasped, but rather grabs us and dramatically "holds" us, expanding the idea of contagion from infection to the more general suspension of the normality of life. But what continues to be basically unpredictable and uncontrollable—even through all the necessary strategies of containment—is our very existence. This time of pandemic forces us not only to come to terms with new, dramatic problems of our individual and social existence but to understand—by living it—that our very existence "is" a radical problem that seeks an adequate response: the problem of happiness—that is, the question of the absurdity or sensibility of our being in the world. What seems different to me, today, is that these questions are once again being posed, albeit confusedly, as a personal task: we can no longer be content to assume that the meaning of ourselves, of our work, of our expectations, of our projects, are clothes or codes provided by the great machine of the dominant culture, which always claims—certainly not disinterestedly—to tell us who we are and what we should desire and achieve in life. Here, today these questions are once again "ours" in the first instance: questions in the first person, that we ourselves have to answer.

But to better understand what is at stake, let's start from the "metaphysical" backlash (if I can call it that) that has marked each of us in this epidemic. It is as if we suddenly became aware of the world that we had inhabited automatically a few weeks before, and we became aware of its presence at the very moment when it—for reasons of emergency and health prevention—became increasingly deserted and threatening, like a theatrical scene from which the actors had disappeared, taking refuge in the wings. And back comes that harassing idea, most often exorcised by a thousand things to do and fill our time: the idea that we are destined to end. It's not a simple "memento mori": we know that one all too well. And it's not even a depressed hypochondria, due to the restriction of our activities. Much more: it is the dawning of the consciousness of our *finiteness*. And it is here that nihilism plays all its cards. Yet in the end it runs the risk of finding itself with no more cards to play.

For the most part, we identify the finiteness of existence with our mortality. But death is not merely the biological cessation of life; it is the most proper dimension with which each of us relates to ourselves and to others, to nature and to history—what Heidegger called the "being-toward-death" that belongs in a constitutive way to our life. It is closely related to the fact that human beings, compared to all other types of entities, have the peculiarity of "being-there" (*Da-sein*); that is, they are never just "what" they are, but what they "can" be. They are always an open possibility. And yet this being-possible of human beings, this opening forward, always includes a falling back, in their "being-thrown" into the world. And this being thrown does not simply mean that we always live in a certain situation of space and time (here and now), but much more that we are irrevocably assigned to ourselves, without reference to anyone to assign us, and without the relationship to someone to whom life in itself would be oriented. Certainly, we have a thousand relationships with people, things, situations, but in our being we are alone, entrusted by no one to ourselves; and this is why we will never be able to realize ourselves, because our being, due to its being-assigned and integrally delivered to itself, is different from that of all other things. We are irreducible to every other entity, but at the same time this irreducibility is what confines us to ourselves as the entities that are by their nature "impossible." Heidegger writes: "This characteristic of Dasein's Being—this 'that it is'—is veiled in its 'whence' and 'whither,' yet disclosed in itself all the more unveiledly; we call it the '*thrownness*' of this entity into its 'there'; indeed, it is thrown in such a way that, as Being-in-the-world, it is the 'there'" (*Being and Time*).

And so, if finiteness is linked to our mortality, as an ontological condition of living as a being thrown into the world that is our own naked self, it means that we are all marked by an insuperable "impossibility." In fact, all our possibilities—projects, actions, transactions, constructions—will never succeed in "fulfilling" our life. A sign of this is the fact that every time we believe that we have achieved fulfillment through the things we have managed to "do," a deeper dissatisfaction immediately arises—tacit or explicit—because none of our achievements can ever fill our desire for happiness. It would be too little.

It is not a coincidence that Heidegger himself (always in *Being and Time*) underlined a phenomenon that will have an enormous success in understanding the human condition of the twentieth century, namely an "anxiety," a sort of disorientation in front of the impossible, where things no longer speak to us, the world refuses to tell us its meaning, and our being fades into "nothingness." And for Heidegger, it is precisely this nothingness that would be the extreme name we can give to the mystery of being, to safeguard it from our subjective representations and from our continuous tendency to identify the truth with the products of our "machinations."

Please note that we are not just talking about abstract philosophers, but about the fabric of our everyday consciousness, about that metaphysical sensitivity to oneself and to the world that moves our experience as conscious beings from within (infinitely wider than our being scholars of philosophy). What does it mean that we are not simply what we can make (of ourselves and the world), but more fundamentally, are consigned to our own "impossibility"? That we are finite beings, certainly. If we stop to think of it, however, the concept of finiteness alludes not only to the fact that we are beings-for-death but also—and even before that—that we are beings who are "born." This is what Hannah Arendt recalled, identifying in "birth" the characterizing trait of our being in the world. Being born is, in fact, not only an event of our past but a permanent dimension of our existence, always called upon as we are to "start" something, to put our possibilities into action, and above all to realize ourselves, not because we are capable of doing so (who is ever equal to being?), but because we have received ourselves as a gift. This reception of self is not in the order of necessity, but rather of pure possibility—on the borders of the impossible. This possibility does not have the seal of thrownness, but rather the vibration of gratuitousness. "It is in the very nature of every new beginning"—writes Arendt in *Between Past and Future*—"that it breaks into the world as an 'infinite improbability,' and yet it is precisely this infinitely improbable which actually constitutes the very texture of everything we call real. Our whole existence rests, after all, on a chain of miracles." The improbable, we could say, is an "impossible" that keeps within itself the permanent trace of possibility, of the event. Miracle is this event, because it is not due, not predictable, not statistically enclosable in a case. And this means that in the series of natural occurrences, every birth is the principle of an irreducible and unrepeatable individualization. Alison Stone made this very clear in her recent *Being Born: Birth and Philosophy*.

Arendt also draws a very significant parallel between the "improbable" character of natural events and the "miraculous" character of human life. The inorganic genesis of the earth, the appearance in it of organic life, and finally the birth of human beings within it, are all processes that, from a statistical point of view, are highly improbable, or even appear to us as "'infinite improbabilities,' they are 'miracles' in everyday language." This miraculous dimension, according to the philosopher, is "present in all reality," and for this reason events, when they happen, "strike us with a shock of surprise." Here is the test of the ontological finiteness of every birth: "The very impact of an event is never wholly explicable; its factuality transcends in principle all anticipation." The miracle here is not arbitrary, artificial, or even superstitious. Rather, it is "most natural and, indeed, in ordinary life almost commonplace." And it is realistic to look for this miracle not even though, but precisely because, it cannot be foreseen. The same cognitive vibration emerges in a letter sent by Arendt in 1965 to Karl Jaspers: "Remaining loyal to reality through good and through ill is what all love of truth really amounts to and all gratitude for the fact that one was born in the first place." Only this gratitude can overcome the anguish about and resentment of the fact that things are gone (Alain Finkielkraut noted this in a beautiful book-interview of a few years ago entitled *L'ingratitude*). But gratitude depends on the realization of being born, of being someone's child—that is, of carrying within oneself the profound promise of the beginning.

Many of us in the terrible days of the *lockdown* had before our eyes the testimony of the many doctors and nurses who literally gave their lives responding to the call for help of their coronavirus patients. But we would reduce this action of theirs by considering it only as a heroic act of will: instead, these people remind us of that gratitude of being born which is like the beginning of the dawn, the light that unexpectedly spreads in the darkness of the trial—of that trial that is life, in its birth every moment.

CHAPTER NINE

SHOCK IN THE FACE
OF MYSTERY

What do we really think about when we talk about "reality"? I am not referring primarily to the theories that lie behind or influence—consciously or unconsciously—our daily discourse. Instead, I would like to start from these discourses and from an observation that is as evident as it is disorienting: the fact that an invisible and uncontrollable virus has quietly but implacably made inroads into our lives, unhinging from top to bottom the order on which, for better or worse, our society was based, opening before our eyes a threatening chasm, as if suddenly a ravine opened at our feet, the bottom of which we cannot see. And we stand on the edge, perplexed and frightened, trying to take all measures not to fall in, but also uncertain of how to overcome it and go on with our "normal" life. Chaos seemed to have taken over the usual world, blowing up habits, relationships, plans, and strategies and forcing us to wonder if what we had experienced up to then—and how we had experienced it—was true, was real, or whether it was just an unstable convention or (even worse) a fragile illusion. At the bottom of every reassurance we hastened to give each other, in the intrusive chatter of the long days of quarantine, there remained a feeling of impotence in the face of the imponderable. Because it is true that, sooner or later, we can come to terms with it; but something similar could still return, every moment, when we least expect it, as a permanent threat on the horizon. The fact is that it is not just an anxious reaction or a psychological insecurity, but a real *shock in the face of mystery.*

In order to understand the meaning of the word "reality" we are forced today to recognize that reality implies by its nature "mystery." And this last word, after a long time, returns to resonate in our perception of the world, saying that reality is other than us, greater than us, unpredictable with respect to our control. Today this seems to be undeniable evidence because this otherness has touched us suddenly, harshly, without our being prepared for it. But for a long time—the time of nihilism, precisely—*mystery* was a marginal and increasingly marginalized word in the vocabulary of advanced societies. Certainly each one of us, from the first emergence of consciousness, has carried and continues to carry within us some perception of mystery, when faced with the fundamental experiences of life: the sweet surprise of falling in love, the undeserved joy of the birth of a child, the bitter drama of the death of a loved one. All of these are mysterious moments that open deep cracks in the apparently compact surface of life, making us suddenly perceive its unfathomable depth, arousing astonishment but also dismay, wonder and fear at the same time. It is that shocking "real" that disturbs and calls into question the routine of a "reality" taken for granted, to use the two terms proposed by Jacques Lacan. We are reminded of this by the unforgettable images of some great contemporary painters, such as the "cuts" on the red canvas by Lucio Fontana or the burnt sacks and "cracks" of Alberto Burri: cracks, cuts, gaps, wounds that show the mysterious dimension of reality and at the same time the real nature of mystery. This is where the visible refers to the invisible and the invisible makes us discover the full extent of the visible.

For a long time, mystery has been confined to the box of the irrational, or what we simply cannot explain. A dark and enigmatic territory in which our mental deductions cannot penetrate. Modern rationalism had tried in various ways to neutralize what exceeds our ability to measure the world, that is, what does not fall within the a priori knowledge of our reason, until finally, in the great claim of positivism, declaring the mystery nothing more than a superstition that science, progressing, would inevitably pulverize. The reaction to this illusory claim has then led, in some moments of twentieth-century thought, to a rehabilitation of the mystery as pure chaos, as the ungovernable irrational, as the nothingness that is always ready to devour us, or even just as the seal of our existential inability. So either the mystery is ousted from the power of reason that measures everything, or it is confined to a sign of the impotence of our reason.

But the crisis of our times—which is also a crisis of nihilism—challenges us to focus on this presence of mystery in our lives and in our knowledge. Only that mystery is harsh, not at all edifying or sentimental: it challenges us to understand the consistency of the world and of ourselves and to discover that there is a *logic* of mystery without which our own rational understanding of the world would hardly function. Isn't this an experience we all have, at least sometimes, when dealing with things? We recognize that reality makes infinitely more sense than our measurements. And isn't it true that when this happens we know *more*, more deeply but also more extensively, about the world? But the question will never be pacified or resolved once and for all. When reason comes to recognize the mystery, there is always a dramatic struggle between our just claims to have the solution of life in our hands and the stubborn provocation of reality. And so there will always be someone—not only outside but *inside* us—who will continue to reduce the mystery to a "sweet dream" (to use the expression of the philosopher of the mind Daniel C. Dennett, one of the champions of reductionism), the result of our emotions and illusory expectations, to which no reality corresponds.

There remains, however, one unresolved point that troubles us, and that is our own consciousness. Our "I" is the most inevitable mystery for ourselves. In fact, today the dispute has shifted from metaphysics to cognitive sciences. For many, the mind is a mystery because we still do not know how our rational and free acts of consciousness are caused by the biochemical processes of our brain. Because after all, as John R. Searle suggested, consciousness is as much a part of our biological nature as photosynthesis, mitosis, meiosis, and lactation ("Reply to 'Searle's Biological Naturalism'"). It is particularly interesting for the theme of "mystery" that an exchange of views occurred, within a horizon marked by "biological naturalism," between Searle and Dennett. Dennett, again in his 2005 book *Sweet Dreams*, on the philosophical illusions of consciousness, compared the path that must be taken to get rid of the (alleged) mystery of consciousness to the one made thanks to the Copernican astronomical theory. To the perceptive observation of each of us, it still *seems*—apparently—that the earth stands still and the sun and the moon revolve around it. Yet each of us *knows* that—in reality—the opposite happens and that ours is only a perceptual illusion that persists. Similarly, explaining the rise of consciousness on the basis of brain mechanisms only will inevitably lead us to consider as illusory a conception of our consciousness as a reality completely different from the biological one, and therefore to see it, compared to the latter, as a "mystery" or a "miracle." In short, consciousness is a phenomenon that can and must be explained "in the third person" ("it"), since the "first person" ("I") is only an illusory oversight. And so, the day will come "when philosophers and scientists and laypersons will chuckle over the fossil traces of our earlier bafflement about consciousness: 'It still seems as if these mechanistic theories of consciousness leave something out, but of course that's an illusion. They do, in fact, explain everything about consciousness that needs explanation.'" Would we ever say, today, that the earth is standing still at the center of the universe? And when we say that tomorrow the sun will rise, we know we are talking about an illusion and we know why it is an illusion, having discovered the actual reality of the motion of the planets. According to Dennett, in a short time—but it seems frankly a prediction that is, yes, quite illusory—no one will be able to say that consciousness is a problem of mental subjectivity of people, once this problem has been eliminated by a mechanistic explanation. Of course, we will continue to say "I," to speak in the first person, but we will know that this is a literary illusion, sweet and perhaps even necessary for living, but in fact incorrect, indeed nonexistent. So far Dennett.

Searle will respond to this "eliminativist" position, stating that consciousness is not worth the process of unmasking an illusion by explaining how it differs from reality, for the simple reason that even when we delude ourselves about something, we are in fact already exercising the activity of our consciousness. It can delude itself, of course; but it is not illusory, indeed it is quite real, that it deludes itself (an argument that the great Descartes had already proposed). "We cannot perform eliminative reduction on consciousness," observes Searle, "because the pattern of eliminative reductions is to show that the phenomenon reduced is just an illusion. But where consciousness is concerned, the existence of the "illusion" is the reality itself. That is to say, if it seems to me that I am conscious, then I am. . . . The "illusion" of consciousness is identical with consciousness" (*Mind, Language and Society*). For Searle this does not mean to propose again the ancient dualism of mind-body. In a previous text, titled *The Mystery of Consciousness*, he had already stated that consciousness is a reality "emergent" from neurobiological processes, in the precise sense that these processes "cause" as their effect "subjective states of awareness and sensitivity," even if we *still* do not know how this happens. One thing is certain: just as the liquidity of water is the result of the movement of molecules that are not liquid in themselves, so the subjectivity of consciousness must be the result of neurobiological factors that are not conscious in themselves. But then "the mystery of consciousness will gradually be removed when we solve the biological problem of consciousness." In other words, when applied to consciousness, "mystery" is not a metaphysical bias that—as happens in other cases—presents obstacles to scientific knowledge of the brain. In this case, "mystery" means that "at present we not only do not know how it works, but we do not even have a clear idea of how the brain could work to cause consciousness. We do not understand how such a thing is even possible. But we have been in similar situations before."

In the reality of our consciousness there is a mystery. Is it only an obvious illusion to be removed? Is it a temporary ignorance that will disappear when we have explained its cause? The fact is that consciousness in some way always mocks its analysts and especially its critics, because it is already at work in those who want to deconstruct it: indeed its deconstruction is the proof of its function. We can ignore, or simply problematize, what kind of reality consciousness is made of, but we are already inside its performing function. This is the mystery of consciousness: it does not depend, negatively, only on our inability to account for our subjective awareness, because on the contrary, the mystery belongs exactly to the sensitive and thinking capacity of our consciousness and is, so to speak, embodied in it.

Gabriel Marcel, in his essay "On the Ontological Mystery," once stated, "A mystery is a problem which encroaches upon its own data, invading them, as it were, and thereby transcending itself as a simple problem." For Marcel, an eminent example of mystery is the problem of the existence and identity of our self ("The *I am* is, to my mind, a global statement which it is impossible to break down into its component parts"). A second example he gives is that of the union of the soul with the body, because already in saying "I have a body" or "I feel my body" I presuppose the indissoluble unity of me and my body. This unity, however, cannot be adequately "analyzed nor reconstituted out of precedent elements. It is not only data; I would say that it is the basis of data, in the sense of being my own presence to myself, a presence of which the act of self-consciousness is, in the last analysis, only an inadequate symbol." Any explanation that wants to detach itself from this consciousness in order to explain it from the outside does not go very far, because the consciousness from which it would like to distance itself in order to analyze and dissect it as a neurobiological find always, in reality, carries all explanations with it. But then where does this persistent capacity of my conscious (and self-conscious) being come from? The mystery is not the failure to answer this question, but coincides exactly with this question itself. It is in the arising of the question that the mystery manifests itself. Its destiny is not so much to be resolved or thinned out, as if it were a fog in front of knowledge, but to remain—through the ever-open question about itself—as the permanent origin of all knowledge. Again, then, we cannot reduce the problem to our measurements: we must reasonably assume mystery in order to understand how biological nature becomes consciousness and freedom, and especially *why it* becomes so. In short, the mystery remains even in all our explanations about "how" reality works. Indeed, just understanding the how of things, we are assailed by an astonishment for the *fact that* they are there. As Ludwig Wittgenstein wrote at the end of his *Tractatus Logico-Philosophicus* (1921), "It is not *how* things are in the world that is mystical [i.e., the mystery], but *that* it exists" (6.44).

CHAPTER TEN

THE DISTANCE BETWEEN CERTAINTY AND TRUTH

What will become of us? In the time of the pandemic crisis—as in every critical situation that affects personal and social existence—this question has come back to haunt us, poignant and implacable. It is heartbreaking because it is the sign of an ultimate tenderness toward us, taking care of our destiny—that is, the possibility of fulfilling or not fulfilling what we desire in life. It is implacable because it is a question to which we are unable to give a predictable or automatic answer based on our intentions or our programs. Indeed, in this question we touch upon the fact that being in the world means always being in question and that life is an adventure—individual and collective—that we must always live through. The only answer we can give to this question, "What will become of us?," is that no one can be sure of what will happen. And it is in fact a creeping uncertainty that is the most rampant, shared feeling in our current condition. But a cultural shift is taking place before our eyes. In the long season of nihilism, of which we are all, to a greater or lesser extent, heirs, certainty was considered by many as a sort of *disvalue*, a dogmatic residue with respect to the emancipation of critical reason, whose task seemed to be precisely that of dismantling all certainty as a dangerous presumption and, ultimately, as an impossible claim. This theoretical position was based on the sincere observation that our way of knowing, always partial and limited, never allows us to grasp the indubitable essence or the ultimate truth of the world. But there was also another reason (perhaps less innocent and more ideological) to support the impossibility of certainty—namely, the conviction that certainty would be only a construction of ours, a psychological, cultural, and social strategy to protect ourselves from the risks of life and the world. In short, to be certain would mean to delude ourselves. This was considered so true that the only possible certainty is that we are not certain of anything. Perhaps the only exception is the one sedimented even in our daily language, when we wish to express absolute conviction about an event or a person, and say that it is "as certain as death." And so, in order to live, we cling instead to the certainties that we construct by our own doing, enclosing ourselves in safety fences or relying on collective narratives.

On the other hand, in spite of this theory left over from nihilism, *uncertainty* has increasingly imposed itself as the real evil in the transition from the twentieth to the twenty-first century. It is what sociologist Zygmunt Bauman has repeatedly described lucidly (for example, in the essay *Liquid Fear*) as a new perception of our powerlessness and contingency after the collapse of the various modern attempts to replace God with other "lords" of our lives. To exorcise this uncertainty, individuals willingly rely on the protection of society and the state, but it is an increasingly disappointed expectation that ends up being thrown back on the shoulders of individuals, now exposed to having to face life's unforeseen events helplessly. Bauman was echoed by another great sociologist, Ulrich Beck, a keen observer of what he calls the "world risk society," in which "the anthropological certainty of modernity" turns out to be "a quicksand" and the individual is charged with the new, heavy responsibility—material and moral—of facing global risks on the basis of his or her own decision (and never before as in our viral time have we understood what a global risk is to be faced through individual behavior). This carries with it the paradoxical consequence that the postmodern individual, the one who pursues as an ideal a "live and let live" mentality, detached from other ties if not from himself, ends up being seized by the panic that the system of security may collapse. And so, far from being his own master, he appeals more and more to the "control rationality" on a political, social, and technological level in order to make "the smooth operation of systems" possible again (*World at Risk*).

The paradox, then, is that precisely in the era of widespread uncertainty, the question of whether there is something or someone of which we are certain reopens in a positive way—and it reopens not as an abstract hypothesis, but as an essential need, something we must have in order to live. And all of a sudden the skeptical theory that identified being certain with being dogmatic shows itself to be simply inadequate for grasping the problem of the existence of contemporary man, as if it resoundingly missed its target. But as often happens, a new understanding of the phenomena constituting the human condition and the words we use to designate them can arise from within a crisis. Usually "certainty" is seen as a subjective experience, unlike "truth," which would instead indicate an objective state of affairs. And for this reason some philosophers have preferred truth to certainty, on the grounds that one could also be certain of things that are in themselves deplorable. In short, the step from certainty to blind and irrational faith would always be lurking. After all, when Hermann Göring, one of the most devoted Nazis, stated, "I have no conscience, my conscience is called Adolf Hitler," wasn't he expressing a (tragic) certainty? In this case, certainty is understood instead as a belief that no longer carries the problem of truth. But it is not enough to appeal to truth to do away with certainty. Let us try to do the reverse, and ask ourselves, What would a truth without certainty be, if not a knowledge without impact and reflection in my existence? Truth, of itself, is independent of our opinions or reactions; however, only when we acknowledge it, when we absent ourselves or dissent from it, does truth become our "experience." Here is the whole kernel of certainty, without which we could not live: the assent that our intelligence—driven by our freedom—gives to the real that comes to us.

The critical problem of a gap between truth and certainty, together with the equally critical urgency of their mutual implication, has emerged in a blatant way in a controversy that broke out a few years ago against the postmodern drifts of hermeneutics. This is the accusation: if there is a gap between truth and certainty, in our knowledge of the world there would never really be objective "facts" with which to come to terms, but everything would be only interpretation, cultural construction, or, worse still, political control in which knowledge becomes "power" and power controls knowledge. In a trajectory that goes from Nietzsche to

Heidegger and Gadamer, and from Foucault to Gianni Vattimo and his "weak thought," the fate of ontology—the "hard" version of an objective reality independent of our interpretations—would be dissolved into pure epistemology. The fuse of this philosophical-political controversy was lit by Maurizio Ferraris, who in turn presented himself as the herald of a "new realism," in which the "inemendability" of reality with respect to our mental schemes also became the key to a truly emancipatory political practice in the name of the objectivity of facts and actual situations in the world—in short, a return to ontological objectivity in knowledge and social action, debunking the postmodern commonplace according to which, by freeing oneself from truth and setting everything up as a hermeneutic perspective, the freedom of rights and opinions would be guaranteed. The new realists retorted that the outcome was populism and fake news. In short, when ideological certainties are in crisis and even hermeneutics risks proposing a weak and problematic version of "certainty" as interpretation (the only certainty is that everyone interprets the world differently), it is time to return to the good, old, reliable truth. This means that we can happily give up certainty, for it is too subjective, unreliable, ambiguous not to risk blurring the true. The point is, however, that we cannot resolve the issue by limiting ourselves to putting facts in the *place of* interpretations. Doing so would basically confirm the dualism between reality understood in its objective "hardness" and our "I," understood as a merely subjective practice. So we would have either facts or interpretations. What if, instead, this return to "realism" helped us—sometimes in spite of itself—to understand the original and inseparable link between these two factors?

Perhaps, then, we should start again from the sense of reality as a "given": something that exists independently of me, but which brings me into play. In my opinion, everything is at stake in the completely open—that is, nonprejudicial—relationship between thought and reality. What is the ever-looming risk of the dispute between "weak" thought, according to which there are no facts but only interpretations, and the "new" realism, according to which there are objective facts that cannot be amended and are independent of our interpretations? On the one hand, to conceive a thought released from the constraint of reality, on the other hand a reality simply independent from thought. One of two things is true: *either* the facts do not allow themselves to be modified, *or* the interpretations claim to modify everything. But in the game of the two positions, it is precisely the constitutive link between thought and reality, or between reason and the world, that is now jammed, so that interpretation remains only a subjectivist "perspective," while the only possible sense of the objectivity of reality is that of being external to the subject. In postmodern hermeneutics, it is as if *I no longer ask anything of truth*, and my freedom is only the beautiful violence of the will, or the (less beautiful) violence of power; in objectivist realism (in which there is a bit of an echo of the old and new positivism) it is as if *truth no longer asks anything of me*, except to be recognized as what I am not. I, on the other hand . . . well, that still remains only the realm of my own interpretations and cultural constructions.

It is therefore a matter of regaining a truth as "mine," to which I can assent with all the affectivity of my reason, *making sure* that this truth is up to the demands of my reason. And it is a matter of permanently questioning our certainties in order to *verify* that they are up to the effective giving of the world. Among those who have most convincingly focused on certainty as an essential dynamic of our intelligence and affectivity is undoubtedly John Henry Newman. Wittgenstein, who quotes him at the beginning of his book *On Certainty*, knew this well. In the *Grammar of Assent* (1870), Newman tells us that human "certitude" is "the perception of a truth with the perception that it is a truth"; that is, certitude occurs when a true thing is not only true but is reached, acquired, consciously assimilated as "ours." The certainty we need is not only an insurance or a guarantee on life, but the trust in something true that we do not make ourselves, that is given to us or that we encounter, but thanks to which we can walk, risk, even make mistakes without losing the path, that is, the goal. Such a certainty cannot simply be contrived or programmed by us; it requires that it be witnessed by someone to whom we can reasonably accord our trust.

The certainty we need is the certainty that a lonely or narcissistic "I" can become a shared "we." And in fact, from the very first glance of our mother when we came into the world, and then on through the decisive encounters of life, the true certainty is always a "you."

CHAPTER ELEVEN

ASK ME IF I'M HAPPY

In the end will we really succeed in being happy? Will the unspoken promise that troubles us, and sometimes gnaws at us, be fulfilled? Or will it leave behind only regret? Happiness is like the deep intentionality in our every gesture, in every act of knowledge, in every initiative. Of course, from time to time we want one thing or another, we aim at certain results, we try to solve particular problems, but that expectation of self-completion is the engine that gives start and energy to our human motion. Normally we look at this expectation for happiness with a kind of modesty, or as Rilke once wrote, with "shame," as if it were "some speechless hope" (*Duino Elegies*, 2). All the effort of human thought, at least in that part of the world in which Western philosophy has established itself, has always aimed at this unutterable realization: and how could one ever define the fullness of life, that is, a satisfaction that is not only of a passing moment, but that lasts forever? Of course, we "nihilists" almost instinctively handle these words with great caution, mixed with skepticism, so great is their claim and so burning is the disillusionment that we have often felt with respect to their promises. So happiness remains as if on the margins of our programs, an unreasonable expectation, precisely because it cannot be calculated. And often, when we have tried to produce it ourselves, happiness has turned out to be an unrealistic, perhaps impossible dream. And to think that the problem of happiness has been the motive for much of our history—personal and cultural—until it was even codified as an "unalienable right" in the American Declaration of Independence of 1776: "the pursuit of Happiness."

The great strategies for happiness of the classical world, Greek and Latin, still shine for their elevation; but the more they shine the more they recede like unreachable, celestial bodies. This does not prevent them from being frequently taken up again as anthropological and ethical models—of an ethics of the limit, of measure and of finiteness—by the neo-pagan tendencies of the nihilistic era (I am thinking of Salvatore Natoli's passionate reference to neo-paganism). And this belies the false belief that nihilism is synonymous with unruliness and libertinism: in the late nineteenth century one could still think so, but then, after the belle époque, with the great century of world wars and totalitarian ideologies, nihilism took on the face of order and moralization. And when, between the end of the twentieth century and our present time, nihilism has often taken on the appearance of relativism, rather than an alternative or a way out of nihilism, the call for an ethic of humanity's self-formation has constituted the other side of the better-known and more conspicuous demolition of the values of traditional morality.

For this reason, referring to the strategy of pagan virtues—considered integrally and exclusively "natural" and still unharmed by the annoying worm of the Christian supernatural—is often assumed as the "constructive" side of the nihilism of our time. How can we not think of the Aristotelian ideal according to which perfect happiness consists in contemplative activity, that is, in the practice of intellectual reflection through which human beings can take their lives into their own hands and make of them a completed work according to the highest image of themselves?—an activity that only gods and philosophers can achieve, because in them the rational nature of life finds fulfillment, that nature that makes us free to see the world disinterestedly, in its necessity and eternity. Recall the famous passage from Aristotle's *Nicomachean Ethics*: "Happiness extends, then, just so far as contemplation does, and those to whom contemplation more fully belongs are more truly happy, not as a mere concomitant but in virtue of the contemplation; for this is in itself precious. Happiness, therefore, must be some form of contemplation." What also comes to mind is the Epicurean counterpoint, or that of an ancient Stoic, according to which a person can be happy only if they can moderate their needs and achieve an absence of disturbance and distress for the soul, "content"—that is, satisfied and at the same time bounded—in their own measures. As in the case of intellectual contemplation, in that of an asceticism of pleasure human beings are called upon to achieve happiness through the exercise of their virtues, or through a defensive strategy. The "Sovran Maxims" of Epicurus's so-called *Tetrapharmakos* give us a significant criterion of the way to happiness as a strategy of self-containment in life: "Don't fear god, don't worry about death; what's good is easy to get, and what's terrible is easy to endure." For Epicurus, a person who assumes these criteria for their existence will find it easy to get rid of what seems—but for them *it seems* only—to be the most serious obstacle to our happiness, namely *the fear of* death. Once the fear is dissolved, the threat of death is also reduced: "Get used to believing that death is nothing to us—Epicurus writes in his *Letter to Meneceus*—for all good and bad consists in sense-experience, and death is the privation of sense-experience. Hence, a correct knowledge of the fact that death is nothing to us makes the mortality of life a matter for contentment, not by adding a limitless time [to life] but by removing the longing for immortality." Happiness is a liberation from infinite longing, from our striving for "forever."

In the pagan world, philosophy served precisely as a kind of "spiritual exercise," according to Pierre Hadot's fortunate formula, or as a kind of "therapy of the soul" (Giovanni Reale has spoken of this extensively) to try to achieve happiness. It is with the breakthrough of the event of Christ and the development of Christian thought that happiness is no longer something that can be achieved through philosophy or other mental strategies, because the grace of Jesus is not revealed in the first instance to "the wise and learned" but "to the little children" (Matt. 11:25). And these little ones are not just the ignorant, but those who have the simplicity of faith; that is, they recognize the coming of the One who can make life happy also, and above all, for those who are not capable of doing it themselves. But is there anyone who can sincerely say that they are?

From this revolution of happiness, understood now as what an Other can accomplish in one's own life, came a fundamental idea for our civilization—namely, that perfection does not coincide first and foremost with the outcome of our abilities, but with the occurrence or gift of something that is far more than we deserve. Try to eliminate from your consciousness and from the narrative of your existence this idea of gratuitousness, and you will no longer even be able to sustain the idea of being happy—nor make the very idea of life bearable. And this is in fact what has happened in those "modern" systems of thought that have wanted to interpret the Christian revolution of happiness in a purely "ethical" sense, as in the morals of Kant, for example. Kant proposes himself as the most mature heir of the Christian tradition, because he recognizes, above the sphere of sensitive and selfish interests, an ideal world of the spirit and of freedom. The point is that this freedom has only one way to realize itself: to obey—as one's duty—the imperative of the moral law that reason imposes autonomously on itself. The law commands "a priori" to follow what is universal—which is attainable by every human being thanks to their own reason—and *not to* follow the individual desire to be happy. Abandoning happiness becomes the price to pay to be truly "moral" human beings. Kant writes in the *Critique of Practical Reason*: "The exact opposite of the principle of morality is [what results] when the principle of one's own happiness is made the determining basis of the will." To be virtuous one must not aim to be happy. Of course, then Kant will somehow recover the concept of happiness. Virtue itself, in fact, is called by him "worthiness to be happy"—that is, not only being "in need of happiness" (this is also true of nonvirtuous persons, that is, those who follow only self-love) but also and above all being "worthy of happiness." Reason could not in fact admit that a person who is worthy of happiness—not because they aim at happiness but *only* because they are virtuous, that is, they follow the command of the moral law—does not then also become happy. For this reason Kant must postulate a just God who, *in a future life,* will grant every person as much happiness as they have merited in their earthly life. But, precisely, happiness is, for morality, only an affair of the future life. In this life duty wins.

This enmity between duty and happiness was one of the fuses that set off contemporary nihilism. Nietzsche, for example, shows, with his usual but lucid interpretive violence, that it is a false alternative: the duty of bourgeois societies, thought without happiness, makes the latter reduce itself to being content with what the social order and cultural standards in vogue have already decided. All this must be destroyed: this is "the hour of your great contempt . . . the hour in which you say: 'What matters my happiness? It is poverty and filth, and a pitiful contentment'" (*Thus Spoke Zarathustra*). Therefore, to save happiness from the world of bourgeois calculation, it must be understood and pursued as chaos and irrational chance, a vitalism without purpose. The fact is that if we detach reason from happiness, we are likely to lose both: one reduced to a cost/benefit planning mechanism, the other reduced to a violent or disillusioned dream (recall the movie *Joker*, directed by Todd Phillips, with the tragic Joaquin Phoenix?).

Certainly, in our time there remains the great alternative to happiness; let's call it "Spinozian" happiness: that which is conquered not through sensible goods, which decay and are always exposed to the cases of fortune, but through the discovery, made through our intellect, that everything is necessary, rigorously concatenated in an iron series of causes and effects. Happiness is realizing that everything is necessary, because everything is nature, and that nature is God. And therefore we can be happy only if we clamorously disprove the illusion of our freedom. "In the mind there is no absolute, or free, will," Spinoza writes in the *Ethics*; rather, "the mind is determined to this or that volition by a cause, which is likewise determined by another cause, and this again by another, and so ad infinitum." Everything is caused, nothing is free; the only joy comes from identifying oneself with the necessary order of the world. Freedom is liberation from passions, not by virtue of superior moral principles but only by recognizing that even the motions of one's own soul, one's own affections, belong to the great mechanical balance of actions and passions of natural forces. And only the wise, the philosophers, can recognize this, and therefore be happy. The end of the *Ethics* comes to mind: "The wise man, insofar as he is considered as such, suffers scarcely any disturbance of spirit, but being conscious, by virtue of a certain eternal necessity [which in fact coincides with God], of himself, of God and of things, never ceases to be. . . . If the road I have pointed out as leading to this goal seems very difficult, yet it can be found. Indeed, what is so rarely discovered is bound to be hard." All this would seem to be the opposite of the nihilistic demolition of supreme metaphysical values, and instead perhaps it constitutes its perfect reverse: both are united by the affirmation of a necessity of the world, which basically means the inexistence of ends and of a meaning that is greater than the world itself. Those who pay attention will not fail to notice that it is precisely the figure of Spinoza that can be glimpsed as the great prompter and inspirer, in the wings of Nietzsche's theater. One thing is certain: for both of them, happiness can be achieved only at the price of freedom, unless we understand freedom as the panic dance that melts in offering to the unstoppable cycle of nature, or as the empty, enigmatic smile of the Greek kouroi, the archaic statues of young people that can be seen in Athens, together with the female figures of the korai: priestesses and priests who celebrate eternal necessity, divinely taking on human troubles.

The fate of happiness thus seems compressed in a vise, between the ethical strategies of self-control and self-fulfillment in life, on the one hand, and the resolution of the individual self in the eternal, divine order of nature, on the other. In both of these possibilities, however, happiness is always something that must be earned or achieved at the end of an arduous journey of a person's intellectual and practical virtues, with the consequence that, understood in this way, happiness loses all interest in existence, and for some is replaced by *moments* of satisfaction—which remain, however, just single and transient moments, without history—and for others, certainly most, happiness is reputed to be simply and sincerely impossible. But then, to return to the original question, will we really be able to be happy in the end? Happiness is *impossible*, and yet at the same time it is *impossible* to live without seeking or desiring it. How can we think together about this double, mutually exclusive impossibility? The only way is for one of these impossibilities to be shown to be untenable. To understand this, it is enough, as always, to pay attention to our conscious experience. Perhaps it is time to stop projecting happiness— thus risking dismissing it—as the outcome of one of our projects or behaviors, and recognize that it is already present—here, now—as part of our lives, as the motor and criterion of our every desire. As Augustine once asked himself, if it is true that everyone—without exception, even those who are sad and discouraged—wants to be happy, where did they know the very notion of "happiness" in order to desire it? If they did not know it in a certain way, they could not even seek it. But we all discover it when we rejoice in something, and this generates a *gaudium*, an enjoyment in our being. This enjoyment is the present trace without which we would not even try to be happy, would not even be oriented and leaning towards the future.

This character of double impossibility of happiness (impossible not to desire it and impossible to produce it) can be illuminated by what Jean-Luc Marion has called an "impossible phenomenon" in reference to forgiveness. And indeed: who would not say that the desire for happiness coincides with or implies in itself the desire to be forgiven? And this not only and not so much as a forgiveness of some specific shortcomings, but of our own limitation, of our finiteness, of the impossibility of self-fulfillment. In short, a forgiveness of the unforgivable (according to Jacques Derrida's precise definition). From this point of view, we could call this notion of happiness one of the "negative certainties" of which Marion again speaks. Negative certainty is that of something that we *wish* to know—our self, God, the gratuitousness of the gift and the event—but that we are *unable* to know because it exceeds the capacity of our mind. Nevertheless, the knowledge of this excess is not less than that of "positive" certainties; we can be certain of objects that go beyond our cognitive possibilities, not *despite* our incapacity, but precisely *because* they reveal it: "Recognizing negatively the 'limits of the mental powers' . . . constitutes, negatively, a certainty comparable to the positive knowledge of any object" (*Negative Certainties*).

Is everything resolved, then? Not at all. Everything is back at stake, rather, because this poses the riskiest question with respect to happiness: Is there something or someone who truly responds to this search? And there is no need to be afraid of not realizing it: if it is the true answer, it can only make the heart rejoice and reason breathe. Augustine, with the acuity of one who has gone through the whole challenge of nihilism, even if it was not yet called by that name, identified it with three simple words: "gaudium de veritate" (joy about the truth; *Confessions* 10.23.33).

CHAPTER TWELVE

THAT DRAWING HIDDEN
INSIDE THE FOG

One of the most peculiar characteristics of human beings—strange as it may seem—is the ability to think of "nothingness." And this is not just a sophisticated theme for professional philosophers, but an experience that has happened and happens to everyone: the perception of emptiness, bewilderment, anguish that assails us at certain times, and of which we can give no reassuring explanation other than that "it was nothing . . . ," while deeper down it was nothingness itself that advanced in our consciousness. Eugenio Montale captured it in a line of acute poetic knowledge, even calling it a "miracle": "Nothing at my back, the void / behind me, with a drunkard's terror" (*Forse un mattino andando in un'aria di vetro*). They are brief moments, sometimes lightning-fast, other times hidden in the folds of existence, which, reverberating from the depths of our living like a "basso continuo," deafeningly accompany our thoughts and our daily occupations. I am not talking about the discomfort of particular psychic cases, but of a widespread and shared condition, which I would not call a pathology at all, but on the contrary one of the most eloquent signs—however enigmatic—of our own "nature." Nothingness is a possibility within the real, which is always in front of us; or rather it reveals itself within us and around us, reminding us who we are and why we are.

In the history of thought "nothingness" has often represented a problematic "focus" in understanding—not denying—being. Let's

80

think, for example, of the "Parmenidean" approach, according to which nothingness is to be thought only as nonbeing or as becoming, the passage of things from being to nonbeing or vice versa, therefore as the opposite or the contradictory to what "is." This is that faith in becoming that Emanuele Severino has called the madness of the nihilistic West. Alongside this position, from Plato onward, other conceptions were immediately affirmed, according to which nothingness is never simply the opposite of being, but is closely involved with the latter. This served precisely to explain the relationship between the identical and the different, the multiplicity of things and, especially with Aristotle, the becoming in time as the transition from power to act. But it was above all the Jewish-Christian conception of creation from nothing (ex nihilo) that gave a new perspective to this concept. It is a new look whereby finite things are conceived as a free gift, because they did not have to be.

Human beings think of nothingness not because they *do not* think of the being of things; on the contrary, they think of nothingness precisely to the extent that they perceive the gift-character/givenness of things, their positive presence. Things are never just "what they are" and that's all. They possess, so to speak, a fourth dimension; that is, they are perceived insofar as they come into being, they are given, they happen in what they are. Things are "given" insofar as they are "events": they are never abstract entities, but historical presences; that is, they happen in their own space and time. This has to do with amazement at the fact that something exists, like the amazement that resonates in Leibniz's famous metaphysical question, "Why is there something rather than nothing?" (*Principles of Nature and Grace*). For some, this question doesn't really make much sense: it is rather superfluous, indeed useless. What could or should ever be "added" to the fact that things are there, ascertained, established, present before us? It is only an annoying habit of philosophers to unnecessarily double an ascertained fact with a rhetorical question that has already been answered, because things are simply there in front of us, ready for the use we want to make of them. This is the ancient objection of "positivism," one of the most resistant forms of modern and contemporary rationalism, according to which things "are" what we are able to quantify, measure, or elaborate through our ideas. It is only our mind that can decide the meaning of things, which in themselves do not tell us anything: mute presences, raw material that we then, following the *patterns* of the culture in which we live, transform into elements for our constructions. So the only certain reality of things is the one determined by the procedures of science: and let metaphysics be patient, but it will have to give up the pretense of making us *know* something other than science. At most it will be able to recycle itself in the role of networking all the knowledge that can be interconnected. There are no more gaps, interruptions, holes or empty spaces: there is no more (the) nothing that escapes from this network.

According to other interpreters, however, Leibniz's question is inevitable, but only as a statement of the fact that something is there, not because it can be answered, since in itself it does not provide for any possible answer. As Umberto Eco stated in an interview granted in 2014 to Antonio Gnoli, "It is not a question to which we can give an answer, or rather whose answer is the very fact that we can ask it. I mean that only someone who is somehow there asks it. To put it in big words, we live in Being and we can ask the question why there is being only because there is being. If there were only nothingness we could not ask the question, but the question is that nothingness does not exist." This question, therefore, is not absolutely irrelevant: "The fact that there is being is the reason why we are led to ask the question and therefore the question has only one answer: 'Why yes,' because if there was not something we could not even think that there could not be." Perhaps the most radical (and please note that we are not making a simple review of philosophical theses, but identifying ways of a person's being in the world, even if not informed by philosophical concepts)—the most radical, I said, are those who have glimpsed in the question of Leibniz a subversion of the way to explain the world by the classical metaphysics—those, that is, that look for a "foundation," that is, a "cause" from which the entities derive and that constitutes the "reason" of all things (in German, moreover, these three terms, "foundation," "cause," and "reason," are all implied in the term *Grund*). It was Heidegger, in a memorable text, *What Is Metaphysics?* (1929) who suggested this reading of the question. In his version, "Why are there beings at all, and why not far rather Nothing?," can be understood (as, according to him, philosophy would have almost always done until then) as a request for a "why" of things. If instead we read the question from the second part of the sentence, "and . . . not far rather Nothing," we realize that the latter, far from being a rhetorical addition to the first part, is actually the enigmatic origin of the question itself. This second half indicates that "being" is not identified with an entity (with a single thing) and not even with the sum of all things, but radically differs from them; it is the "different" or the "difference" itself that is precisely, compared to the entity, the "nothing." This means that things cannot be explained by an entity that acts as a cause, because its foundation (*Grund*) is actually a nonfoundation (*Un-grund*), or even a bottomless abyss (*Ab-grund*). And this means that being remains as a mystery that in turn does not find explanation and foundation on our part, but is the pure "giving" of things; an origin that cannot be reached, but only thought of as a retreating and at the same time a granting, a refusing and at the same time a giving.

Certainly, Heidegger had probably drawn this insight from the Christian conception whereby God is the very being who originates his creation as a free gift. But when, according to him, this origin was identified as a "cause" and creation as an "effect," the mystery of being was lost. It became a necessary law. Therefore, it must be rethought as a gift without a donor: the gift from nothing and of nothing. Hence an acute interpreter such as Luigi Pareyson has taken a further step: to call this nothingness "freedom," not in a moral sense, but as a free movement, not as a necessary cause that produces its effects according to certain principles, but as the truth of things that is not another, superior thing. And God himself would no longer be the necessary entity that founds all reality, but would come to coincide with this same freedom, close to "nothingness." Nothingness, therefore, does not simply mean the no-being of something that existed before, or the no-being of what will still exist, but constitutes a dimension proper to everything that is or that can be, its "origin," the trace of its coming into being, of its happening. Nothingness is therefore not an empty concept, indicating what remains when everything is annihilated or there is nothing more. On the contrary, it is a concept, so to speak, full of being, which allows us to grasp in things the trace of their origin, both in the sense that this origin itself is given and in the sense that it withdraws from our grasp. For everything—including myself—not only was wrested from nothingness at the beginning, but in nothingness affirms itself every moment of its existence. Even *now*, in what is here present, nothingness is not an outdated residue or a dialectical negation with respect to what is there, but is the persistence of the mystery of the presence of everything present. And here everything changes according to what we see: we can see a present thing *only* as the set of its determinations, as the outcome or the effect or the product of certain determining factors, or we can perceive its presence more as a movement of coming to me than as the goal of what is in front of me. In the first case, things reset nothingness to zero and that is enough; in the second case, things carry within themselves, *themselves*, the memory of nothingness.

On the other hand, nothingness is a concept directed not only toward the past but also toward the future, as much twentieth-century philosophy has understood, thinking of what is specific to human existence: it means that human beings are "open" beings, who can never be fulfilled because they are capable of freedom, or condemned to it (as Sartre would say). Therefore we are transcendent beings, always open to possibility, to what is not yet or could be otherwise than the necessity of nature. Nothingness here therefore means the "transcendence" and freedom of human subjects. But what is most interesting is that in front of this nothingness, consciousness and the very perception we have of ourselves are at stake. Put more simply, nothingness can open the door to recognize the abysmal gratuitousness of being, due to nothing else but, so to speak, its intimate grace. On the other hand, nothingness can also close that door to make us surrender to the absurdity of our existence and of the world. In other words, thinking of nothingness, we can safeguard the mystery of being with respect to our representations and our strategies, which always aim to reduce being to an entity that is at our disposal; or we can simply conclude that everything that exists cannot have any other ultimate meaning than nothingness. Therefore—as Heidegger states—the human being can be seen as "lieutenant of nothingness" (again from *What Is Metaphysics?*) and thanks to this can become the "shepherd of being," "being called by being itself into the preservation of being's truth" (*Letter on "Humanism"*). But human beings, subjects capable of consciousness and freedom, as Sartre pointed out, have the peculiarity of always denying being. And for man, therefore, to be free would mean "generating nothingness" in himself and around him.

It is significant that for both authors I am talking about, nothing-ness is always an experience linked to the state of mind of anguish and to the discovery of a deep "nihilation" (*Nichtung, néantisation*)—only that while for Sartre anguish is the very sign of being free on the part of human beings, who are condemned, as we said, to nihilate their own being, in Heidegger, anguish on the part of being is the place where all things vanish into disorientation and nothingness, as an "entranced calm" offers us—precisely because it repels us—the deepest understand-ing of being. The scenario then extends and is enriched if we consider (as was recently argued, for example, by Zhihua Yao) that the way in which Heidegger thought of nothingness distances itself from the West-ern philosophical tradition to get much closer to the Buddhist one, and in particular Taoist. Nothingness thought here is, to use Kantian termi-nology, neither *nihil negativum*, which "cannot be" at all because it con-sists in a logical contradiction (like a square circle), nor *nihil privativum*, as "absence," that is, as negation with respect to anything positive (evil with respect to good, shadow with respect to light, cold with respect to heat). In addition to these two meanings, referring respectively to Par-menides and (neo-)Platonism, the nothingness can be thought of instead in a third way as *nihil originarium*, and in this sense is identified with the being itself as disclosedness of the world and entities. This "original nothingness," of which Heidegger speaks, is the same found in the mil-lennial Taoist tradition, perhaps drawn precisely from the reading of the *Tao Te Ching* of Lao Tse by the German thinker. Nothingness, then, as "the source or origin of all existents," is a true "cosmogonic" provenance.

The interest that these voices always hold is such as to go be-yond mere philosophical theory and rather offer possibilities for a self-understanding of life. And several times it can happen that they help us to realize just how much an intuition or a word is evocative of meaning, able to illuminate a knot of experience, even if we were not at all "follow-ers" or supporters of the general philosophical doctrine of those who sug-gest it to us. It seems strange, but we must recognize that the problem of our relationship with reality is played out—in one direction or another—precisely in the field of nothingness. And so we must perhaps in some way reappropriate this nothingness, go through it, let ourselves be dis-turbed by it and provoked by it, without being in a hurry to liquidate it and thus "give it away" to nihilism. On the contrary, I would say that it is precisely by going to the bottom of the call of nothingness, by understanding what it asks of us, that we can contribute to overcoming contemporary nihilism. As was rightly noted by Michael Novak, "Nihilism is an ideological interpretation imposed on the experience of nothingness" (*Experience of Nothingness*). And it is once again a great "nihilist" who understands what is at stake. I am talking about Virginia Woolf, and in particular about one of her autobiographical writings dating back to 1939, but published posthumously under the title *Moments of Being*, in which we can feel an unprecedented and "positive" vibration of the problem of nothingness. Here literary experience becomes one of the clearest and most precise ways in which existence understands itself. Our days, Woolf writes, are made up of "moments of being," which nevertheless "are embedded in many more moments of non-being." Reality is a "goodness" that, however, is "embedded in a kind of nondescript cotton wool." We could call it the wadded bunch of meaninglessness, of the lack of a living and experienced meaning for oneself and for the world. And so "a great part of every day is not lived consciously." But Woolf goes on: it is only thanks to a "sudden violent shock," to "exceptional moments" in which something "happened so violently that I have remembered it all my life," that in that wad of stuff a sudden gash opens "for no reason that I know about," and things become transparent, finally showing themselves as "real." These moments can be marked by "despair" or by "satisfaction": in the first case a sense of absolute impotence wins; in the second case one feels that what is happening can be "explained" by discovering it as a "revelation": the sign but also the *token* "of some real thing behind appearances." Hence a philosophy or, at least, "a constant idea of mine; that behind the cotton wool is hidden a pattern; that we—I mean all human beings—are connected with this; that the whole world is a work of art; that we are parts of the work of art." In those moments, Woolf concludes, "poetry was coming true" and "the pen gets on the scent." Indeed, "I go on to suppose that the shock-receiving capacity is what makes me a writer."

What does it mean that the poem becomes true, real, if not that meaning becomes embodied, becomes incorporated, becomes recognizable by our reason and desirable by our affection? Moments of being are truly such—we all experience this—because each time they are not taken for granted or automatic, predictable and programmable. They are, after all, "snatched" from nothingness, and we can experience them in the muffled circle of our mechanisms, or feel the miracle of their presence. Of this nothingness pierced by the presence of things, events, and people, nihilism paradoxically knows nothing. It deals exclusively with managing, measuring, and calculating reality "technically," depriving itself of the need for an ultimate meaning of itself and of the world. Nothingness—as a concept but even more as an irreducibly human experience—can then be seen as the point on which to leverage, to overturn, the great claim of nihilism. Nothingness is perhaps the greatest friend of being.

CHAPTER THIRTEEN

ON THE DESIRE
FOR TRUTH

There was a time, in the history of modern nihilism, when "truth" had become, almost without realizing it, an embarrassing word in public language, and undoubtedly annoying in private language. The very concept of truth in the common imagination was loaded with a claim that was barely bearable, so cumbersome was it: the reference to an absolute, binding, unchangeable vision of things. It is enough to think of how the appeal to a truth constitutive of human nature or to the ideal truth of a political value almost always met with the objection that, in reality, it was a question of a particular position or choice passed off illegitimately as universal. Of course, in this type of objection, the often hidden driving force was the one dictated by political circumstances and ideological perspectives. Accordingly, the same factor in some cases was considered a false "truth" constructed on the basis of the precise interests of just one part of the population or governments, and in other cases it was presented as an indisputable truth. There is no shortage of examples, at least on the Italian and European scene: from the flow of illegal immigrants from North Africa to the possibility of homosexual marriages; from the lawfulness of disposing of the end of one's own life or that of one's loved ones in the absence of certain conditions of "quality" to the obligatory or arbitrary nature of vaccinations, all the way to the recent discussion on a law against homophobia and for the recognition of the "gender" and not merely "biological" identity of persons.

But in recent decades we have seen that the grand project of freeing oneself from the individual and social burden of truth, making way for a system of multiple but not overlapping interpretations of the world, has often entailed a risk of return that contradicted the expectation of liberation. It is the risk of liquidating reality or reducing it to what power—of whatever kind, from that between people to that in society or economic life—decides it to be from time to time. Truth has always, in fact, an enormous social weight, but I would say not only in a negative sense (a risk that has been present many times in our history, when someone has decided what is real and what is not according to his ideological schemes) but also and above all in a positive sense, as a safeguard and defense of the freedom of people against the violence of prejudice. The turning point today is under everyone's eyes through the murky issue of "fake news" and the media's ability to deviously orient consensus and the very perception of the world. Precisely through the planetary dominance of technology, according to which nothing is "given" anymore, all reality can be tendentially created and controlled by those who hold the monopoly of digital information—often linked to the interests of the world's political and economic powers—and talking about truth becomes no longer a duty, but an irrepressible need for freedom. In reality, the preparation of this kind of linguistic and conceptual embargo of the concept of truth has been very long in coming and, as we often find out, the widespread nihilism of our time is the outcome of a process that developed slowly within the history of thought. But never before as clearly as in this case can what has happened in the course of Western philosophy be traced in the events of our mind—as if we used a pantograph and traced the great lines of the culture of the last centuries in the daily folds of our being in the world.

There is an experience that particularly marks modern thought with regard to the problem of truth, the one described by Descartes in his *Discourse on Method* (1637) when he recounts his deep dissatisfaction with the teaching he received at the Jesuit College of La Flèche based on the disciplines of the "scholastic" tradition, precisely because they did not provide him with a sure criterion for recognizing truth. Because of this, he decided to set out on a journey to discover "the great book of the world." And he notes: "I constantly felt a burning desire [*an extrême désir*] to learn to distinguish the true from the false, to see my actions for what they were, and to proceed with confidence through life." It is significant that for Descartes the driving force of the search is a desire that he calls "extreme," because it is like the tension of every other problem in philosophy and life: the desire for truth, to be able to understand, to touch reality in its truth.

At the beginning of modernity, truth becomes a problem again, beyond traditional solutions, because it reasserts itself as a desiring act on the part of human beings. This is the sign of truth: that it is desirable, and that is a need that the "I" has, to exist and realize itself. In short, truth is a problem of life. And we have truth only to the extent that we seek it, desire it, tend toward it. Certainly, starting from this initial point, Descartes made his way and developed a method that would ensure the most controlled and firmest possible possession of the knowledge of the world, such as that managed by mathematical analysis. But that initial move has always continued to fascinate and question me, and paradoxically has allowed me to pose critical questions to Descartes himself: Did his identification of the truth of the world in the sign of a great machine that could be explained geometrically as a series of quantitative relations between quantities, with no other possible ends, succeed in satisfying the entire breadth of that original desire for truth? That is, did it exhaust all the truth that was in question in the restlessness of the I?

When two centuries later Nietzsche answered this question in a decidedly negative way, he was forced by his iconoclastic radicalism to demolish the very concept of "truth": "I was the first to discover the truth, by being the first to sense—smell—the lie as a lie. . . . My genius is in my nostrils. . . ." ("Why I Am a Destiny," in *Ecce homo*). This can be strange, in light of the fact that Nietzsche is usually presented as the great demolitionist, the one who first dismantled the concept of truth. But he was able to do so precisely because he felt once again, in all its irrepressibility, the problem of truth. The beginning of the crisis of the twentieth century, a crosscutting crisis in the most diverse practices and disciplines, from mathematics to literature, from physics to psychology, from art to historiography, lies in the fact that truth becomes a problem. The formula is ambiguous because it does not so much state that there is no more truth as that the *problem is truth*, because it has lost its evidence.

But the crisis does not annul the initial question; indeed it reopens it: Where does this desire come from, a desire that now, precisely because it is unsatisfied, is charged with violence? This is the reason that Nietzsche puts into the mouth of the wanderer, the protagonist of his thought: "One day the wanderer slammed a door shut behind him, came to a halt, and wept. Then he said: 'This penchant and passion for what is true, real, non-apparent, certain—how it exasperates me! Why does this gloomy and earnest oppressor follow me of all people!'" (*Gay Science*). Why does the traveler cry? Because he feels hounded by the problem of reality, by the need for truth that he would like to flay off his skin, so importunate is it, a hindrance that does not allow him to "build himself up" as he would like. It is something like the force of gravity, but at the same time it makes him angry: he feels its absolute urgency, without being able to account for it. And in fact, for the "nihilist" Nietzsche, this desire must be almost eradicated and the "I" of the finite man, searching, desiring, must go beyond in the "superman" or "beyond-man," and his desire must amplify and distort itself beyond measure in the pure will to power, according to which everything is true because everything is necessary, and the "I" is only a bourgeois residue to be left to its decadence.

Certainly, this is another Nietzsche compared to the one who has been handed down by postmetaphysical thought (some call him postmodern), champion of interpretations that win over facts, of relativism that wins over the objectivity of reality, of extreme perspectivism in which everyone is called upon to construct his or her own self. Our Nietzsche, on the other hand, is a little different, poised between two extremes that he himself has allowed: on the one hand, the liberation of the drives of the modern subject (in the name of his hero: Voltaire), finally freed from truth; on the other hand the identification of freedom with the entirely "Spinozian" acceptance of the great necessity of the world, in which everything returns eternally the same. Between these two extremes, Nietzsche's problem remains unresolved. And it is the one that allows us to understand how the nihilism of our time has changed compared to his. It has changed because the two-solution hypotheses we have just seen have *not* succeeded—as they basically promised themselves—in no longer perceiving the problem of truth. On the contrary, their inadequacy in the solution has relaunched the sharpness of the question.

Truth cannot be thought of from a detached self, liberated from reality; nor from a necessary reality, without the freedom of the self. Truth lies in the relation between them. The relation is its problem, because it is not to be thought of merely as the sum of two addends each already constituted in itself, but as the way in which each of them is *true* thanks to the other. As all those who think of truth as what emerges in the judgment of knowledge know, to grasp the true means (according to the famous canon of Thomas Aquinas) to surprise the correspondence or the adequation between our intellect and reality (*adaequatio intellectus et rei*). We *are* true and we live *in* truth not because we never make mistakes or are never in error, but because we are already always in the manifestation of reality. We are in the truth because, even in error, we "are" in relationship with the real. And the real "waits," if we can say so, for our openness to manifest itself in its true sense.

There is a simple, but I think effective, example that I often give my students to help them recognize this state of affairs of the truth, of our self opening up to the truth of the world. Let's say you fall madly in love with a person, and they don't reciprocate at first, with the obvious consequence of your deep sadness and dissatisfaction. But then, with time, and maybe with a bit of luck, the situation changes, and the other person falls in love with you, returning your affection. The evening you find out, everything changes and at night you can hardly sleep, so much so that this new love has "taken" you. In the morning, as soon as you wake up, what is the one thing you will probably do? Call or meet that person and ask them, explicitly or tacitly, "Tell me it's true!," or, "Is it really true?" Each of us is made to enjoy that affection, and together—and in this togetherness the whole game is played—we are made to enjoy its truth. This affective need for truth implies a question, not casually but constitutively, because it is a truth that can never be reduced to something already known, just as affection needs to be renewed and deepened always. Bruno Latour described it with another example that fits well with the one just given, in his book *Rejoicing, or The Torments of Religious Speech*. "Imagine a lover who answered the question 'Do you love me?' with this sentence: 'Yes, but you already know that, I told you so last year.'" One could even imagine that the answer to the question had already been recorded on a tape recorder and that it was enough to press the replay button to listen to it again. In reality, this would only mean that those who refer to an answer given (and even recorded!) in the past have stopped loving in the present. But there's a problem: "The fact is his girlfriend didn't ask him if he *had* loved her, but if he loves her *now.*" It is not enough, therefore, to repeat word for word the sentence already said a year earlier in order to express the same truth in the present. Or on the contrary, one may not repeat the same sentence but make it true through a gesture or a glance: "And so it isn't the sentence itself that the woman will closely follow, or the resemblance or dissimilitude between the two instances, but the *tone*, the manner, the way in which he, her lover, will revive that old, worn-out theme." This means once again that truth is not reduced to simple information about things, but constitutes a way in which things happen, and happen again in time. It is not an informative discourse, but rather a *performative* one, in which, that is, what is enunciated happens (and for Latour this is the specific feature of the language of love as well as that of religion).

I found a better glimpse of the vertiginous scope of this simple example when I came across a passage by the great Swiss theologian and philosopher Hans Urs von Balthasar. In a capital work of his entitled precisely *Truth of the World* (1985) he states that to ask whether, in general, there is such a thing as truth is similar to the question a young man asks his girlfriend, asking her if she loves him. But it is not enough for him to ascertain her love as a mere "fact." "No, this fact, like a door springing open, becomes the starting point of a newly beginning life of love. In this life, the eternal question of lovers—'Does he or she love me?'— . . . is revived every day; love can never be questioned enough, because love never has enough of hearing the reassuring affirmative reply. Behind every answer there is a new question, and behind every reassuring certainty there is an expansive new horizon." Truth is never, strictly speaking, an absolute to be possessed; it is rather, surprisingly, something that has happened, that touches us.

CHAPTER FOURTEEN

THE DUTY
THAT ATTRACTS

One of the salient features of societies marked by the culture of widespread nihilism is a crisis of the recognition of duties, that is, of those fundamental values to which—a little or a lot—a social coexistence must refer in order to continue to exist. With a term that is perhaps not entirely adequate, it is customary to refer to this disturbed atmosphere of our societies with respect to duties as a tendency towards "relativism." This does not mean, however, as traditionalist ideology suggests with a certain petulance, that people no longer have values in which to believe or have simply given up searching for and elaborating a meaning to life. The fatigue of nihilism—which is then also its most challenging and most fascinating side—consists in the fact that the ultimate motivations for existence are no longer recognizable for the universal ideality they immediately express thanks to their supraindividual character (as was more easily recognizable in other epochs). Rather, they are more easily recognizable thanks to whether or not a value corresponds to the expectations and desires for the self-fulfillment of individuals.

And it is no longer just a question of what, with an effective formula, the great sociologist Max Weber had already called the "polytheism of values." In an era of the "disenchantment of the world," "alien to God and bereft of prophets"—Weber argued—the different values remain in constant conflict with each other, and every person is called to pursue an ethics of responsibility, that is, to respond personally to the consequences of their actions. But today, in the epochal passage from polytheism to the "relativism" of values, it seems that the relationship has been reversed: the focal point is not so much the duty of each person to be responsible to society, but the right of each to have their need for individual affirmation recognized by society. This gives the term "relativism" a more just and precise meaning: not so much, or not above all, the disqualification and relativization of principles traditionally considered as absolutes, but the conception of values insofar as they relate to the interests of individual persons, therefore "relative" to them. It is values that depend on people, not people on values. This is why the age of realized nihilism essentially conceives of itself no longer as an age of duties, but as an age of rights.

This of course has entailed—like any cultural polarization that loses the whole complex of experience—considerable problems of conception that have become increasingly evident in the timeline from the late 1960s to the present day. I will mention just two emblematic ones. The first is of an anthropological-social order: if the basis of human coexistence is the (sacrosanct and inalienable) rights of each individual, what happens if there is a conflict between different rights? Let's take some of the most scabrous examples, in order not to simply skirt around the problem: the inalienable right to self-determination of a woman who, on this basis, chooses (with all the personal drama that this entails) to terminate a pregnancy and the opposing right of the unborn child to come into the world. Or, on the contrary, the right to have a child by a person who could not have one biologically and who therefore resorts to surrogacy, as opposed to the "natural" right to experience their own motherhood of those who carry out gestation on behalf of others, as well as the right of the child to be able to recognize its biological mother. Or the example of the right to no longer identify a person with her biological (sexual) nature, but to identify her only with the "gender" she "feels" herself to have. But as often happens, the most acute and interesting problems are the philosophical or even "metaphysical" ones. There is no shortage of them in this society of rights. The most evident is this: that we no longer think of an "I," of concrete flesh-and-blood "subjects" to whom rights are inherent, but we think of rights that produce the subjects that carry them. The claim that a state, through its laws, can guarantee the tendentially unlimited rights of categories of individuals brings with it the idea that it is that legal protection which grounds the reality of the individuals who benefit from it. We do not start from data, but from law. It is not the personal datum that requires, in order to be realized, the recognition of one's own being; rather, it is this recognition that is the source of the person's being. The most relevant cultural and political consequence is a certain pulverization of the fundamental motivations of a social community, which does not stem from a shared motive out of which it can articulate the differences and contrasts between various individual and collective rights, but from a continuous transaction in the dialectics of rights that come to affect all aspects of people's lives. This made an attentive observer say that "we cannot think of recipes from the past, all focused on the unlimited expansion of rights, to the point of making simple desires become rights. A new sense of life can be guaranteed only with a policy of duties. It is duties that give a meaning to life, not rights; yet today few, perhaps none, speak of duties" (Luciano Violante).

Yet, let's face it, "right" is a very attractive term, unlike "duty," which is rather sad. Even in our everyday language duty is something that we have to do, but somehow in spite of ourselves, in spite of what we would like to do. Let's try to think about it: the sedimented meaning of this word takes us where we would not like to go, precisely because we feel obliged, bound, ultimately forced. But why? In one of the most extraordinary "metamorphoses" of the human spirit in search of liberation, mentioned by Nietzsche in his *Thus Spoke Zarathustra*, there is that image of the lion fighting the dragon: "Who is the great dragon whom the spirit no longer wants to call master and god? 'Thou shalt' is the name of the great dragon. But the spirit of the lion says 'I will.' 'Thou shalt' stands in its way, gleaming golden, a scaly animal, and upon every scale 'thou shalt!' gleams like gold." Nihilism is in some way the failure of Kant, of the Kantian duty that has no other motivation than the imposition of duty in itself. Why should one follow duty? The only answer is because one must, that is, because the universal reason present in all individuals commands it. This for Kant is the highest thing that exists in a human being, the worthiest of admiration and "respect": his pure freedom. An absolute end in itself, unconditional. All other things are made as means to something else, or are the effect of some mechanical cause. Only this one, however, is absolutely pure, and pure it must remain: on pain of losing the human.

How is it possible then that such a loftiness was assailed by the nihilistic lion? Perhaps Nietzsche, in his polemical fury against the accursed dragon of "Thou shalt!," which eats life in the name of abstract values, did not see the problem fully—namely, that in all probability nihilism had already penetrated under the scales of the great reptile. In fact, in order to raise the human being to a being as unconditioned as that of the pure moral law, it had to be detached from what a human being "is" in reality and be projected into an impossible "should be." The rational man "can" fulfill himself, is able to realize his virtue only on the basis of his own powers of moral consistency, for the sole reason that he "must" do so. But in this way the man who *is* ends up succumbing to the man *who must be*. Charles Péguy once wrote that man formed by the Kantian ethic of duty—or, more succinctly, "Kantianism"—"has clean hands, but no hands [*a les mains pures, mais il n'a pas de mains*]. And we, our calloused hands, our gnarled hands, our sinful hands, we sometimes have full hands." This conception of duty grasps at nothing: in fact the virtuous person must mortify their sensitive desire, such as the desire for happiness, which is inevitably a particular, individual, private interest. For no one can be happy in my place. The superior desire is only that which aims at virtue—that is, to make oneself worthy of being happy. But it is precisely here that, paradoxically, the problem that will later erupt in nihilism is already born in Kant. And it arises precisely from the fact that there is a separation between duty and sensible desire or the desire to be happy. Following this approach, which is still dominant today—even in those who perhaps for this very reason reject the system of duties and emphasize the system of rights—duty must always be pursued in some way at the price of self. This carries with it the consequence that the particular interest of the individual is in itself morally impure, and therefore suspect. In principle, a self-interest is something that must be stripped away in order for one to become virtuous. Here is realized the great, and also problematic, Enlightenment idea of a universal duty, as detached from individual interests: sublime idea but inevitably, literally abstract.

The problem of duty and the problem of nihilism here seem to partly overlap. This in some way makes any attempt to overcome nihilism, through a renewed appeal to the ethics of duty, an attempt with a blunt weapon. This is certainly not because the latter are not important, indeed unavoidable, but simply because they no longer have any persuasive force. They have in some way already lost the battle before entering it. Precisely because of the way we think of them, duties have now become devoid of appeal. For this reason, it is perhaps worthwhile to repropose a simple question, one that cannot be taken for granted: How do duties arise, in the life of a person, but also in the great history of our culture? For all of us as heirs of Kant (even if we are anti-Kantian!), duty is first of all thought of as the effort of our will that must come to "perform" a certain obligation. But if we think about it more carefully, starting from our own experience or from our personal history, we may find that duty actually emerges from a root that comes *before* our effort. Duty is like the warning that something or someone is calling us: whether it is Yahweh on Mount Sinai, or the voice of our conscience, or a moment in reality that strikes us and involves us, so much so that it moves us. And recognizing this call coincides with our "here I am," as if to say "this matters to me," "this is for me." The origin of duty is not primarily an effort on our part to conform to a superior but distant value, but rather it is an attraction, even a fascination—and this even when the appeal challenges us, awakens us, corrects us.

Let's think of a child, perhaps the child we once were: How can they learn duty? Only because their parents impose it on them as an imperative? But in this case the ideal would only be self-control by a superego, and teaching duty in this way would in many cases mean producing repressed or neurotic children. It will be said that a child can learn duty only because their parents set an example for them. Of course, but parents can make mistakes, and what about in this case? How disappointing to see a parent make a mistake and, by making a mistake, undermine the value they teach. Or perhaps duty is recognized precisely because it arises from the child's own relationship with his or her parents—even if they make mistakes—that is, from the simple fact that "I'm sorry to make my mom cry" or "I'm doing this because I'm sorry to displease her." It is clear that in this way we are at a level in which there is not yet a full awareness of value, and therefore we rationalists would immediately be ready to discard or overcome this root of the learning of value because it would still be "childish," not rationally aware and responsible as in adults. And yet in this example, it is as if the structural root of duty emerges, not just the initial or immature impression of it, but its permanent aspect . . . ? The reason why we learn that this value is a value that is respectable in and of itself—and therefore we can and must universalize it—is that in following that value as a duty, we find that our mother's sorrow comes back to our memory as an indelible matrix: and we would like anything rather than for her to be sad; that is, we would like to correspond to her affection for us. This does not mean remaining sentimentally attached to childhood; on the contrary, it means being able to grow up as grown-up people by accepting duty as a loving invitation to be ourselves: just as those who love us look at us, without pretending we're something we are not.

This very crude hint, very banal if you will, of a daily phenomenology of education to duty, has its *pendant* in the history of our culture. Human beings have not self-produced these values, but have learned them in certain historical experiences, thanks to belonging to certain gatherings, frequenting certain places, certain community contexts, being educated by someone—and then little by little they have discovered that it was worth it, because of the intrinsic rationality of those commands. The great Enlightenment scholar Lessing, in his very famous booklet *The Education of the Human Race*, provokes us again, because he says that at the beginning of history, people needed to be afraid in order to learn duty. And so from Asian polytheism they passed to the Mosaic revelation and to Jewish history, with this terrible and jealous God who ordered and punished. But it was just a step in the education of humanity. Then came Jesus, who taught love and gave the example of what it means to follow the will of a Father. And now, having arrived at our time—Lessing's time, the eighteenth century, but many would still say so now—we no longer have any need for that education, because we have now become adults, and reason can now generate its values on its own. In this respect, nihilism helps us to discover the somewhat vague incompleteness of Lessing's great rationalist project. It is not so: humanity has lost just those values that it had to found autonomously in itself, and that education is not something that is behind us, but in front of us. The root of duty is both a fascination and a belonging; it is a sonship—that is, a sociality, a community.

Charles Taylor, one of the voices most sensitive to the crisis of modern individualism, once wrote: "If authenticity is being true to ourselves, is recovering our own 'sentiment de l'existence' [Rousseau's name for our most intimate contact with ourselves], then perhaps we can only achieve it integrally if we recognize that this sentiment connects us to a wider whole. . . . Perhaps the loss of a sense of belonging through a publicly defined order needs to be compensated by a stronger, more inner sense of linkage" (*Malaise of Modernity*)—because the community is, in fact, that reality in which we are educated to recognize the charm of the most essential duty to which a person can be called, and feel it finally completely "his" or "hers": the duty to be oneself.

CHAPTER FIFTEEN

THAT EMOTION THAT DWELLS IN REASON

Inside Out

"Do you ever look at someone and wonder, What is going on inside their head?" With this question begins one of the most debated films of recent times—in fact, a "simple" animated feature film produced in 2015 by Pixar about kids and (apparently) for kids, which, however, thematizes nothing less than the dynamics of our relationship with reality. *Inside Out* asks the question, What is the relationship between what is "inside" of us with what is "out there"? In what way do things, events, and accidents touch and disturb the mechanisms of the mind? And how do emotions more or less always condition our knowledge of the world?

The story told in the film is that of an eleven-year-old girl, Riley, who after a happy childhood spent in the warm embrace of a caring family, playing hockey on the frozen fields of Minnesota, has to move to San Francisco (for her dad's job) and face the emotional trauma that this change causes in her: first of all the new, ugly house, and then school without her old classmates, and even the pizza bought at the diner down the corner, topped incredibly with broccoli! But the real location of the film is Riley's mind, observed—as in a dissection—in the mechanism of cerebral processes. And the real protagonists are actually not the family, but the *feelings*, the five emotions that stir in this mind—a sort of Platonic cave—and that answer to the names of Joy, Fear, Anger, Disgust, and Sadness, who are personified as cute little elves whose colors, attitudes, and grimaces represent these psychic and neuronal energies, positive or negative, triggered from time to time by the course of events. These are precisely the "primary emotions" mentioned by evolutionary psychology, for example in Robert Plutchik's book entitled *The Psychology and Biology of Emotions*. The mind is portrayed as a large archive of stored data, rendered in the film as spheres of different colors depending on the emotional coloring with which we have perceived the individual moments of our existence. These spheres come and go along the viaducts of the nervous system and cluster from time to time in those floating "islands" in Riley's mind where she builds (but can also collapse) her sense of things through her own state of mind. There's the island of family and the island of friendship, the island of honesty and the island of ice hockey and even the island of silliness—all of which together delineate the girl's individual personality. When the pieces of data in the memory are detached from the emotions, they become flat and geometric, like abstract thoughts, while when the memories become illusionary, they end up in the black abyss of the subconscious.

But the story comes from afar. According to the old empiricist doctrine of David Hume, the Scottish philosopher of the eighteenth century, which is the basis of many contemporary theories on the mind, what we know of the world is never the world itself, but our subjective reactions—sensory and emotional—to the movement of bodies that affects us from the outside, or even to the internal movements of our spirit. But not even our individual "I" exists in the true sense, since it is only a bundle of perceptions held together by habit, made of memory (by which we remember what we have experienced) and imagination (by which we foresee a similar state of affairs). So, as Hume writes, "Let us chase our imagination to the heavens, or to the utmost limits of the universe; we never really advance a step beyond ourselves." The "Self" would then be like a theater in which an ever-changing and different representation takes place; the screenwriters of *Inside Out* would rather call it a "control room," in which a narrative is formed—the story of life, like a Hollywood-style "Dream Production"—piloted by the five *feelings* that push buttons and raise or lower mechanical levers to induce reactions, control attitudes, and seek a possible or impossible balance each time.

Hume was opposing a great author of the seventeenth century, Descartes, who had theorized that emotions (he called them the "passions of the soul"), although they make us "vibrate," "tasting the most sweetness in this life," cannot, however, influence the objective knowledge of the world, which is limited to the geometric-mechanical measurements of scientific knowledge. And from then on, this mentality has become predominant, until today, a "rationalist" image of knowledge devoid of feelings and subjective evaluations, too unreliable to ensure the objectivity of the world, is commonplace. What do these two positions, Descartes's and Hume's, have in common, albeit from opposite perspectives? The risk of a separation between the cold rationality of knowledge and the warm emotionality of feelings. One may prefer one or the other (not only at the level of philosophical theories but also in the different moments of our lives), but the fact remains that one always seems to drive away the other. Yet if we look more closely into the dynamics of our daily experience, we notice at least one point of contact between these two phenomena: when something strikes us, the more intensely it strikes us, the more it constitutes an invitation to *understand what it* is about, to judge what it really is, to know it.

Talking to various people about the film, but also scrolling through various comments in Italian and foreign newspapers, I have observed that two reactions are the most widespread: some (I am thinking of Antonio Polito in the *Corriere della sera*) rightly observe that the screenplay of *Inside Out* lacks reason, that faculty which is in charge of guiding and orienting feelings, allowing them to be conveyed in judgment and knowledge. Poor Riley is entirely "played" by her emotions, without ever being a truly conscious person and, above all, free and responsible in this game of the quintet. Others, on the other hand (such as Julian Baggini in the *Guardian*), hail the film's staging as the one most in keeping with recent neuroscience discoveries, in which the "I" or "self" is constructed from time to time in a narrative induced by emotions and assembled by memory, but without being anything "permanent" or stable. In short, to put it more simply, for some people the young girl in the film is an individual without reason, reduced to her sentimental reactions; for others, however, it is necessary to take note of the fact that at that age (but only at that age?) adolescents are just like that, sucked in by their emotions. It seems to me that the film's interest lies in raising a question about what happens in our experience as people who are in the world: Is our reason an abstract faculty that is added (albeit as a "guide") to our emotions, or is it from the beginning a reason *embodied* in our bodies and in our feelings? And are the latter only instinctive mechanisms, or—allow me to venture—do they already have in themselves the trace of a meaningful judgment, as a point of possible personal "freedom" within the conditioning of emotion?

Certainly, no adequate theory of emotions today, in the perspective of cognitive science and thanks to the progress of neuroscience, would limit itself to considering them only as reactive phenomena of an exclusively physiological type. Emotions are rather seen as processes or models of the elaboration of responses to internal or external stimuli, in which there is not only a reactive passivity but also an adaptive and organizational activity of neuronal elements. An activity—this is the point that interests us most—that goes from the unconscious level to the distinct feeling of what one is feeling, up to the awareness and judgment of it. But then, the cognitive picture widens even more, discovering, for example (as is widely shown by the research of the neuroscientist Antonio Damasio, especially in his famous book *Descartes' Error*), that emotions play a decisive role in the use of our rational faculty, and especially in our decision-making skills. These experimental evidences allow us to reconsider two extreme positions that hold the field in this nihilistic era: for an attentive observer of experience, neither of them can be valid alone, because each always necessarily implies the other one as well, but in the collective imagination it is often given to consider them alternatives. On the one hand, we have the objective world, outside us, measurable by scientific rationality; on the other hand the world inside us, the subjective *feeling* with which we perceive ourselves. The first level of reality would be what is *as it is*, implacably, inevitably, because it is independent from us, from our tastes, our perceptions, our opinions. The second level, on the other hand, is never what it is, but is what we *think* it is or *feel* it is, yet suspended, as it were, from the variability of subjective opinions. But we could also say it this way: the world goes on indifferently with respect to us, following an evolutionary logic that has no precise ends or recognizable purposes, if not those of a development of adaptive reactions to environmental impulses. There are not goals but only necessity or, at most, randomness of events. The world "is" like this. But ends and purposes, without which it is not possible for human beings to live, are no longer to be found in the sky of fixed stars, as transcendent motivations, but as elaborations of our perceptive and inevitably subjective feelings. If we then go on to examine the reflection of the most radical reductionists, such as Richard Dawkins, the hypothesis that is advanced with respect to the distinction of these two levels is that even in the second, no less than in the first, there is a necessary evolutionary determination, so that the biological laws of natural selection would preside over not only the organization of nature but also that of culture.

It is really interesting—and also a bit disturbing—to see the way in which the vision of the relationship between the human being (also called "I") and reality has "evolved." From humanity being considered the perspective point to which all nature and history concur as to their main purpose, in a trajectory that goes from Judeo-Christian creationism up to its secularized form in the Enlightenment idea of progress (let us remember that still for Kant the ultimate goal of creation is man as a moral being), we arrive at the evolutionary self-determination of the whole of reality, in which biology is assumed as the matrix of the same rational and spiritual "nature" of humanity. Once again the philosophical problem of nihilism seems to be reversed into its opposite. At the beginning, it seemed a great possibility of human liberation to emancipate the world from ends transcending the world itself, as if someone who was accustomed to commensurate with a purpose always beyond himself, without ever being able to truly achieve it, came to say: "But I am what I am." I no longer need to look for a "design" or a "plot" for me to represent; I am a transient moment of evolution, and the only meaning that is truly adequate to me is what I emotionally "feel" about myself. But doesn't this emancipatory liberation from finalistic superstructures always run the risk of having as its only direction that of pandering to the most binding evolutionary determinism? But then, is an emotion only a reaction to a physiological stimulus? Or maybe it is just an emotion, which we thought to be on the "passive" side of perception compared to the activity of reason and conscious will, which can open from within an ir-reducible question. If it is true, as our starting philosopher David Hume had clearly stated, that the "Self" does not exist, that it is not a datum, a thing, a substance at all, but only a "bundle of perceptions" bound by memory and imagination, then *who* is it that binds and remembers and imagines? Around whom does the perceptual bundle gather in unity? Is the self just a fluid emotional process without permanent consistency, or do our very emotional, sentimental, and passionate processes attest that there is "something" or "someone" at work? Accepting also the challenge of not presupposing this "subject" with respect to its functioning, but starting only from the latter, does not this very function attest to the imminence and finally the entry of an unknown guest? The guest of the "I" in ourselves, an "I" that surprises us, almost takes us from behind, attested to by our own perceptions.

Try to revise in the light of this hypothesis the *climax* scene of the film, in which Joy, who up until then had been doing her utmost to color all of Riley's experiences yellow-gold, trying to impose optimism on her at all costs, understands that the "positivity" of life is something else and that she cannot annul or censor the blue of Sadness, because Sadness is in fact the secret heart of joy, that expectation of infinite fulfillment that we cannot avoid, but neither can we fill. This friendship between Joy and Sadness allows us to look at and face even the difficulties of life as a step toward our own personal fulfillment. And isn't it true that sometimes we are seized by a nostalgia that is not only the lack of something we experienced in the past but the desire or yearning for something that vibrates in the present, like the voice of a promise of life from which springs the feeling—and at the same time the consciousness—of our "I"?

CHAPTER SIXTEEN

WITH WHAT EYES WE LOOK AT THE WORLD

What happens when we see the reality around us? A perceptive act such as that of seeing has always been considered in the history of thought as one of the moments and places where above all the game of our being in the world is played out. Of course, seeing still does not tell us everything: how many times do we look without really seeing what we are looking at, and how many times can seeing be partial, cut off by a certain more or less narrow perspective, illusory or deceptive? And yet, it is a fact that sight has been assumed since Greek philosophy as the prototype of the understanding of reality. As Augustine notes in a justly famous passage in the *Confessions*, the seeing of the eyes is also used as a term for the other senses when we use them to know. And so we will never say "hear how it shines" or "smell how it shines," or "taste how it shines" or "touch how it shines," whereas we will certainly say "see how it shines," and we will also rightly say: "see how it sounds, see how it smells, see how it tastes, see how it is rough." Sight, however, not only is directed at the world that is outside of us and around us, but also—and perhaps above all—is an inner sight. This is not only because when we hold in memory and imagination what we have seen outside of us, things become ours, but also because we can see the world and ourselves directly inside of us. Precisely because of this, it is in the scope of "seeing" that the whole challenge of contemporary nihilism is also played out, which can be said to depend largely on the answer we give to the question of what we see and are capable of seeing when we look at ourselves and the world. Here nihilism loses its charge as an ideological option and is called to account for itself as a perceptive act.

But in order to make this verification, I willingly start from an author—Italo Calvino—who has acutely grasped the secret nihilistic tendency of our time, catching it in its deepest register: the cognitive one. In one of his famous *Charles Eliot Norton Lectures* dedicated to "visibility" (to tell the truth, not one of the most commonly quoted), Calvino proposed this definition—as fascinating as it is enigmatic—of the chosen theme: "If I have included visibility in my list of values to be saved, it is to give warning of the danger we run in losing a basic human faculty: the power of bringing visions into focus with our eyes shut, of bringing forth forms and colors from the lines of black letters on a white page, and in fact *of thinking* in terms of images." This is why the writer speaks of a true "pedagogy of imagination," which would help cultivate our inner images, preventing them from being reduced to an empty reverie, and instead fixing them in memory as "self-sufficient" forms of representation, which precisely let us see even with our eyes shut. Why does the writer speak of visibility as a value to be saved? It is not simply a matter of a humanistic-literary heritage to be defended for the survival of our cultural world, although for Calvino literature is a metaphor and supreme expression of awareness of the world of life. The question is more radical and concerns the power of seeing something "with our eyes shut," that is, of forming images in one's inner world, not in the sense of an arbitrary fantastic universe, but as the formation of the iconic structures of our thought. The inner visibility of images—or in other words, the ability to see images with the eyes of the mind—constitutes the fundamental linguistic structure of human thought as such. Here Calvino does not seem to me to be speaking only of specifically literary thought; rather he helps us illuminate what we would call the "literary" or "visual" form of all thought and all kinds of thought. This form, according to the great writer, arises from several elements: "direct observation of the real world, phantasmic and oneiric transfiguration, the figurative world as it is transmitted by culture at its various levels, and a process of abstraction, condensation, and interiorization of sense experience, a matter of prime importance to both the visualization and the verbalization of thought."

It is precisely in this indissoluble link between images and words—whether we start from one or the other—in which the exercise of thought consists, that the profound crisis of "meaning" that characterizes our era is gathered, almost condensed, as it is intercepted by Calvino. And probably it is precisely in this awareness of the crisis of modern culture that we find the key to better understand his insistence on "visibility." In one of the essays contained in the collection *The Uses of Literature*, Calvino speaks of the "challenge" of literature and states that it consists in understanding the world in an increasingly analytical and detailed manner. But at the same time it also consists in "a dissuasion from understanding it," since the world reveals itself to be "essentially impenetrable" ("Cybernetics and Ghosts," in *Uses of Literature*). Literature "does not recognize Reality as such, but only *levels*," and more radically, it does not know the different levels of reality, but rather "recognizes the *reality of levels*." Literature moves from one level to another, as in a game in which first "we have witnessed the disappearance of the 'I'"—that is, the first subject of the writing—and then at the end the "ultimate object," or precisely the reality itself that we wanted to know ("Levels of Reality in Literature," in *Uses of Literature*).

On the one hand, literature has an analytical-cognitive scope because it has to describe things, but at the same time, the ultimate goal of this knowledge is to communicate that the world is essentially impenetrable. Therefore, while on the one hand there remains a sort of disillusionment with the fact that reality is ultimately incomprehensible, on the other hand, "the problem is precisely that of being aware of one's own relativity, of becoming master of it, and knowing how to deal with this relativity" (letter to Mario Motta, July 1950). Literature, in short, must teach us to have a good relationship with our own cognitive failure. Or again, in his ingenious and geometric rewriting of Dumas's *The Count of Monte Cristo* (contained in the 1967 collection *T Zero*), Calvino writes: "The only way to escape the prisoner's state is to know how the prison is built." And this is what he himself would later call "my epistemological testament" (letter to Giovanni Falaschi, November 4, 1972). This is the only thing that can be given cognitively, namely writing as the only alternative to the petrification of reality. In the most famous of the *Charles Eliot Norton Lectures*, the first one, Calvino will instead oppose to that same petrification "the idea of lightness" or rather "that particular and existential inflection that makes it possible for Shakespeare's characters to distance themselves from their own drama, thus dissolving it into melancholy and irony." This is the impressive documentation of how the question on the meaning of the self and of reality, which constitutes, so to speak, the incandescent core of the crisis that crosses the different fields of knowledge and life in the twentieth century, comes to bend, to curve in the tacit admission—full of melancholy and irony—of the impossibility of meaning. And it is as if this impossibility took on the physiognomy of a new canon to face and cross—precisely with lightness—the crisis, understood as a permanent and insuperable condition of the subject. Like when, for example, in Calvino's *The Baron in the Trees*, the great illuminist, perched on the branches because he wants to see how things are going from above, at a certain point falls in love with Viola and thinks that he almost wants to come down to go to her. In the end he chooses to stay up there, even though he feels all the "thrill" of his choice, converting it "philosophically" into mental analysis, which continuously aims at recomposing the discarded elements, the unexpected, the irregular excesses of reality.

In the light of these traces, it is perhaps possible to view with greater awareness the level of the question opened up by the Calvinian defense of visibility. A vision with eyes closed—it has been said—an inner vision that structures thinking in images: Isn't this a sort of "curvature" of visibility into imagination and of imagination into a mental vision that must *close* its eyes *in order to* see? Certainly, Calvino appropriately reminds us that the visibility of something is fulfilled at the moment in which its image becomes an integral part of our "I," of our thought. And this happens not simply because we store, as in an archive, the images acquired perceptually or elaborated fantastically, but because we see (and preserve, structuring it) the possible meaning, the reference to its deepest possibility of signification. On the other hand, a few years before his *Lectures*, Calvino himself had focused on the whole problem, or rather the unresolved aporia of looking at the world on the part of the human being. In *Mr Palomar* he wrote: "But how can you look at something and set your own ego aside? Whose eyes are doing the looking? As a rule, you think of the ego as one who is peering out of your own eyes as if leaning on a windowsill, looking at the world stretching out before him in all its immensity. So then: there is a window that looks out on the world. The world is out there; and in here, what is there? The world still—what else could there be?" In short, the ego is also a piece of the world that looks out on another piece of the world. The world is on both sides of the window. But then, "perhaps the I, the ego, is simply the window through which the world looks at the world. To look at itself the world needs the eyes (and the eyeglasses) of Mr Palomar."

But this solution of the problem—the self looking at the world, the world looking at the world—actually solves it by simply doubling it. At first Mr. Palomar thinks that all the things closest to him and all the gestures most familiar to him connect to celestial bodies and cosmic events, as between the lighting of his pipe and "the explosion of a supernova taking place in the Great Magellanic Cloud." But when he then believes he can "apply this cosmic wisdom to relations with his fellows," something "does not work" anymore, because in order to deal with other human beings it is necessary to start "involving himself, and he no longer knows where his self is to be found." The lack of self-knowledge prevents the knowledge of others. But the fact is that "Palomar, who does not love himself, has always taken care not to encounter himself face to face." The last purpose will then be to devote himself to getting to know himself, to explore "his own inner geography," because if it is the world that looks at the world through the self, then "the universe is the mirror in which we can contemplate only what we have learned to know in ourselves." But here also arises the last, most disenchanted disappointment of Mr. Palomar: when he "opens his eyes" he sees nothing but what he sees every day: "streets full of people, hurrying, elbowing their way ahead, without looking one another in the face, among high walls, sharp and peeling." And this makes him discover another universe: no longer the realm of a harmonious celestial mechanism, in which the motions of the stars are guided by the same destiny that has "the ego as its center and its center in every point," but "a stalled mechanism," an "endangered universe, twisted, restless as he is" (one might say as an adumbration of the passage from classical physics to quantum mechanics, to relativity and the uncertainty principle).

Here is Calvino's enigma of visibility: on the one hand, the inner vision—the memory of an image—is like the inner fold of the real, like the "lining" of the world; not in the sense of its hidden foundation, but of its possibility, or rather of its possibilities, which escape the necessity of the actual being and the immodifiable presence of things. But on the other hand, this inner vision only doubles the externality of the ordinary world, already always seen and known, which neither enlarges nor contests, but simply mirrors the interiority, which in the face of what is outside itself functions as the impossible. Vision with eyes closed is like a possibility that distances itself from or subtracts itself from the necessary real, even by simply "imagining" it, and thus encloses, indeed produces within itself, a permanent *impossibility*. Ultimately, in the latter, the only possible meaning of the world would be given—literally, in fact, "impossible." This brings to mind what Theodor W. Adorno wrote about the function of the "aesthetic" as an antithesis with respect to the existing, a distance from the principle of reality: "In each genuine artwork something appears that does not exist. . . . The appearance of the nonexistent as if it existed motivates the question as to the truth of art. By its form alone art promises what is not; it registers objectively, however refractedly, the claim that because the nonexistent appears it must indeed be possible. The unstillable longing in the face of beauty . . . is the longing for the fulfillment of what was promised" (*Aesthetic Theory*).

On the one hand, then, there would be reality with its intolerable weight; on the other hand, the aesthetic experience as an antithetical moment, but precisely for this reason also liberating with respect to the actual being: and liberation would coincide precisely with the promise, even if it is the promise of a nonexistent, and therefore ultimately of an impossibility of fulfillment in reality. So much so that, as Adorno himself observes, "nothing guarantees that [art] will keep its objective promise." And that happens because "even radical art is a lie insofar as it fails to create the possible to which it gives rise as semblance." For Calvino, it is a question of saving the value of the "visibility" of the inner gaze, of vision *with eyes closed*, in order to save the creative irreducibility in the face of a reality, so to speak, condemned to incontrovertible identity and irreversibility.

What if instead, to turn his own terms on their head, imagination and even fantasy were the way to see the world *with open eyes*? The world is given to us in vision, but our vision is never just an automatic "feed-back" of the given; it is rather the essential way—not just the accidental occasion—in which it is *given* in presence. The vision and the giving of the world are the two sides of a single phenomenon. Visibility is precisely the phenomenon in which presence and vision interpenetrate, where the presence of the real becomes visible and our seeing allows the world to be what it is, to become itself. The impossible sense of the world becomes possible precisely when we look at it.

CHAPTER SEVENTEEN

THE LOSS OF THE EGO, THE RECONQUEST OF THE SELF

Nathan Zuckerman is the unforgettable protagonist—and *alter ego*—of some of the novels of Philip Roth, the great American writer who perhaps more than any other has engaged in the feverish adventure of describing what a personal identity is. This Nathan, then, once said, speaking of himself: "All I can tell you with certainty is that I, for one, have no self, and that I am unwilling or unable to perpetrate upon myself the joke of a self. It certainly does strike me as a joke about *my* self. What I have instead is a variety of impersonations I can do, and not only of myself—a troupe of players that I have internalized, a permanent company of actors that I can call upon when a self is required, an ever-evolving stock of pieces and parts that forms my repertoire. But I certainly have no self independent of my imposturing, artistic efforts to have one. Nor would I want one. I am a theater and nothing more than a theater" (*Counterlife*, 1986). These few lines are perhaps worth more than many speeches on the crisis of subjectivity in the contemporary world, and they outline something like the prototype of the nihilistic self that runs through all of us inhabitants of this time, regardless, of course, of the ideological options or cultural beliefs or moral (or amoral) tendencies we may have. This posture of the ego remains a crucial problem, even in spite of all the declarations about its dissolution. It is an easy and cheap operation, on the part of many analysts, to declare the extinction of the ego as a reality of its own, irreducible to its instinctive mechanisms and to the phantasmagorical game of its own self-interpretations. It is very easy, because it gives us the illusion of having freed ourselves from its problem. Instead, it is precisely as a problem that the ego becomes interesting and inevitable. And those who deny it actually exercise their "subjectivity" in a massive way (even if in a self-destructive mode), without really coming to terms with it.

How can we fail to notice—to stay with Roth's self-description—that it takes in any case an "I" with a strong personality to be able to distance oneself in this way from oneself and to be able to deny oneself? Never before has the questioning and deconstruction of the self been the most resounding attestation of the self (and Roth knows this very well). However, when the "I" tries to reach self-consciousness, it seems that it can no longer stand up to itself, in the twofold sense of this verb: it cannot *support itself*, it cannot identify itself as grounded in itself, as someone identical to itself—as a *me ipsum*—but at the same time it cannot *stand up to itself* either; that is, it cannot accept a structured individuality that is not continuously fractured and permanently fluid. It does not accept being something more than what it feels about itself. By what right, the "I" would seem to say, can I attribute to myself a reality that I am not able to create autonomously and to assure myself of permanently? It is therefore necessary to take seriously the nihilistic critique of the "ego" as the "subject" inherited from modern thought, as the one who disposes fully of himself and at the same time conquers the world outside himself by grasping it with his concepts. Taking this critique seriously, however, does not necessarily mean sharing or confirming it, much less considering it a necessary destiny. Rather, it means understanding the question that moves it and some new questions it makes possible.

Almost at the same time as Roth wrote *The Counterlife*, Daniel C. Dennett, in *Consciousness Explained* (1991), took up the idea of the self as a theater of consciousness, to further dismantle it as an illusory image—as illusory as the concept of the self itself would be. Dennett calls the "Cartesian Theater . . . a metaphorical picture of how conscious experience must sit in the brain." In Descartes, the center of this entirely mechanical scene of consciousness—I would say just like a ba-roque theatrical machine—was occupied by the famous pineal gland, the unitary point toward which the stimuli of the external world flowed and from which the counterstimuli of the conscious ego flowed. It is already very interesting that when Dennett speaks of the "ego" or of conscious-ness for Descartes, he no longer refers—as we would expect—to the soul or to the thinking substance (*cogito, res cogitans*) separated from the body, but already to the bodily version of the physiology of the "self." But even this corporeal version must be abandoned, because it presupposes that there is a center, an apex point—in short, a "self" (however physical-mechanical) to which all the gears of the conscious life of human beings are referred. As a substitute for the Cartesian Theater model, Dennett proposes his model of consciousness as the "multiple drafts model." Ac-cording to this model "all varieties of perception—indeed, all varieties of thought or mental activity—are accomplished in the brain by parallel, multitrack processes of interpretation and elaboration of sensory inputs." This is an exquisitely biological strategy, which we (but we might ask: Who? Those we conventionally call *Homo sapiens*) have in common with the spider and the beaver, the hermit crab and the Australian gardening bird. Only in our case, "our fundamental tactic of self-protection, self-control, and self-definition is not spinning webs or building dams, but telling stories . . . about who we are." Thus "our tales are spun, but for the most part we don't spin them; they spin us. Our human conscious-ness, and our narrative selfhood, is their product, not their source." So, all of a sudden, we are talking about a cultural script about one's "self," a mere *fiction*, you might say, because in reality there are only biological processes, not a *biological self*, and likewise there are only psychic pro-cesses, and even the "psychological or narrative self is yet another abstrac-tion, not a thing in the brain." It is only a "center of narrative gravity" simply *postulated* by us, while in fact nonexistent.

Is this radical reductionism in the face of the ego exclusively proper to the nihilism of our time? Perhaps, but not really, if what we read in a writing of about 350 years before is true: the human race is "noth-ing but a bundle or collection of different perceptions, which succeed each other with an inconceivable rapidity, and are in a perpetual flux and movement. . . . The mind is a kind of theatre, where several perceptions successively make their appearance; pass, re-pass, glide away, and mingle in an infinite variety of postures and situations. . . . The comparison of the theatre must not mislead us. They are the successive perceptions only, that constitute the mind; nor have we the most distant notion of the place, where these scenes are represented, or of the materials, of which it is compos'd" (Hume, *Treatise on Human Nature*, 1740). The self is a verbal fiction; literature is the true ontology of the self; creative writing the authentic phenomenology of consciousness. And the theater itself is not even the seat of staging, it is not the *stage of* fiction, because it too is illusory as a place. Pure representation in which there are only characters and no interpreter, pure script without a stable scene and without a playwright (can't you hear the restless echo of Pirandello?).

In the trajectory that goes from Hume to Dennett, it is again the unfailing Nietzsche who centers the problem, in a posthumous fragment dating back to the years 1885–1887: "Against positivism, which halts at phenomena—'There are only *facts*'—I would say: No, facts is precisely what there is not, only interpretations. We cannot establish any fact 'in itself': perhaps it is folly to want to do such a thing. 'Everything is subjective,' you say; but even this is interpretation. The 'subject' is not something given, it is something added and invented and projected behind what there is.—Finally, is it necessary to posit an interpreter behind the interpretation? Even this is invention, hypothesis." And it is interesting to note that this "extension of the domain" of interpretation (to mimic a title by Houellebecq) finds its inversion in the mechanisms of biological evolution intended as a canon to explain—and thereby liquidate—the problem of the ego, much more than in the deconstructive hypotheses of postmodern culture.

This is perhaps one of the most widespread and shared matrices of the nihilism of our time, present across cultural positions also very different from each other. The weakening of the "self" is, in the eyes of many of us, a critical stance at the philosophical and cultural level: a distancing that, to many, seems inevitable because of the undue claims of the "modern subject" and from anthropocentrism as a real system of power, for which everything—nature, other people, other cultures—would be progressively reduced to the claims of the ego, understood as an individual subject or as a collective and political subjectivity. Weakening the subject, conceiving it no longer as an absolute substantial reality, but as an interpretive practice always liable to redefinition, seemed to be the duty of the most conscious and ideologically emancipated culture in the seventies and eighties of the last century (one of the most significant references, in Italy, but not only, was undoubtedly Gianni Vattimo). But this weakening also had and still has a definitely meta-ideological side, in that widespread feeling of living that, since those years and up to our days, has spread in an impressive way among people (especially in the younger generations), and that in a simple way we could define as a sort of asthenia of certainty. Of course, it is not a matter of particular psychological conditions, always present in the personal stories of each of us, but of a more structural difficulty in assuming oneself as a present fact, as someone who always has to prove to him- or herself and to others that he or she is there. As if the starting point of existence was not presence, but the absence of self, to be filled or transformed or constructed as presence. And this passage has two sides: the commitment, or rather the duty, of performance to arrive at presence as the success of oneself, and in light of this, a subtle sadness because no realization can achieve, in the end, a presence that was not already there at the beginning.

But this is precisely where the twist happens. It has seemed to us that the loss of the "I"—whatever way one judged it, as an impoverishment or as a gain—was a typical experience of the nihilism of our time. But now, starting not so much from opposing explanatory theories, but from our own experience, nihilism appears to us instead as a wound of awareness or a noetic thrill *within* the self itself. An "I" no longer seen as the empire of the subject, but as a phenomenon that constantly needs to be reaffirmed with respect to nothingness. It is not that the "I" is lost in nihilism, but on the contrary, it is by crossing and going beyond nihilism (even if most of the time it does not have this name) that the "I" can "be" itself.

Let us try to listen to what an author more than sixteen centuries distant from us tells us about the "self," an author who certainly does not belong to the canon of the "nihilists," but who experienced in a very precise way this dimension of nothingness *in the* "I." I speak of Augustine of Hippo. For him, the human being never "is" properly and absolutely himself, as only God can be. Rather, the "I"—like all created things—tends toward nothingness, even runs toward nothingness: "So when things rise and emerge into existence, the faster they grow to be, the quicker they rush towards non-being" (cum oriuntur et tendunt esse, quo magis celeriter crescunt, ut sint, eo magis festinant, ut non sint; *Confessions* 4.10.15). And the experiential reverberation of this "nihilistic" condition of the "I" lies in the fact that when Augustine speaks of his own self, insofar as received into being from the divine You, he almost always speaks of it as a dramatic event of loss and alienation, which always, however, finds within itself a countermovement of ontological recovery: I am "fruitlessly divided" (frustatim discissus sum), and I have "fruitlessly divided" (in multa evanui) (*Confessions* 2.1.1). The "I" is a continuous *defluxus*, a dispersion and a loss of self, a slipping into nothingness; but the consciousness of this critical condition of the "I," the very realization of this dissolution, can arise only in the gathering of the "I" in its own self. This is the Augustinian concept of *continentia*, which is not the moral experience of *abstinentia*, abstaining from the temptations of the flesh, but rather a *collision*, precisely the movement of gathering from being-dispersed to being-one. But this movement is never autogenous; it is not produced by itself, but is excited by one who is other than itself. In the "abyss of human consciousness" the ego can remember itself because it makes present—in itself—"oneself as another" (according to the beautiful title of a great work by Paul Ricoeur).

But how is it that the "I" perceives itself as a movement toward nothingness that returns to being each time, because the direction of consciousness is reversed? Is this, as mentioned earlier, just another "uplifting" story (like dams for beavers)? Is it just a narrative strategy by which biological evolution self-delimits and self-defends in the face of what is beyond and outside itself? The beauty of the nihilism of our time is that we cannot take the answer to this question for granted, and above all we cannot spare ourselves the question. Every form of reductionism actually tries to solve the problem of the self by eliminating the question, that is, by denying the fact that it is a problem. But in this way we do not take a step either in the exploration or in the experience of the "I," for the simple reason that the "I" is itself the problem—a problem that reopens (never to close definitively) every time we perceive things.

I was very struck by the way a psychiatrist such as Oliver Sacks talks about it, because he attests, from within the very interior of a decidedly naturalistic perspective (tied with a double-strand to biological evolution-ism), to the inevitable emergence of that problem. In one of the writings published after his death in 2015, titled *The River of Consciousness*, Sacks argues that our brain is not a rigid system, but is continuously subjected to an "experiential selection," in the sense that it is precisely experience—and therefore consciousness—that shapes "the connectivity and function of the brain." Even experience can modify the brain, as we can see, for example, in the case of our vision of something, which is explained by the fact that a continuity of consciousness happens, dynamically linking together—as in a film—static frames, snapshots, in a single sequence. Consciousness, in short, is composed of discrete moments, which in it and because of it become a *continuum*. "But we deceive ourselves if we imagine that we can ever be passive, impartial observers. Every percep-tion, every scene, is shaped by us." This is not a voluntary, conscious de-cision, but a posture, I would call it, of the observer. This is why "we are the directors of the film we are making—but we are its subjects too: *every frame, every moment, is us, is ours.*" And the question is inevitably raised: How is it, asks Sacks, that we can achieve a continuous flow, in which the individual moments are not dispersed but are linked together? Only because each of our thoughts "bears the brand of this ownership," which is precisely the mark of our ego (*as its Self*). Then "our very being" is not *only* made up of "perceptual moments," simple physiological moments, "but moments of an essentially *personal* kind."

But isn't the personal brand of the owner of my thoughts—that is, my own self—a sign that what we wanted to explain as the *apparent* correlate of a neural mechanism is *indeed* that without which this same mechanism could not even give itself? In short, we always come *too late* in wanting to prove the biological determinant causes in the emergence of the self, because they simply already imply it, require it, accompany it. And it is reasonable to assume that the whole analytic-experimental procedure aimed at the reduction of the self to its neurobiological func-tions may, on the contrary, constitute the most resounding proof of its presence.

CHAPTER EIGHTEEN

AN AMBIGUOUS POWER

The Technical Face of Nihilism

If we wanted to identify the characteristic traits of the nihilism of our time, we would certainly have to look for them in the *technical* order of the world. After all, it has been like this since the times of the first, great nihilistic explosion of the twentieth century, in particular in what Nietzsche—as mentioned—identified as a nihilism no longer "passive," but "active." Just think of the lucid, ruthless analysis of an exceptional observer such as Ernst Jünger. Starting from the progressive transformation of the human being in the function of "worker," a profile of humanity not only social but, so to speak, metaphysical, and also taking into account the advanced technological mechanization of war conflicts (already in the First World War, understood as "war of materiel"), Jünger had sensed that the deepest sense of nihilism was not to be found in the spiritual weakness of *décadence*, but in the militarily organized system of society. He identified nihilism not in the illness caused by the decline of the old values, but in a new health—more precisely, in a new "physical health," arising precisely from the loss of an ultimate sense of reality that was not the pure functioning of a system of order. In other words, the nihilistic condition would not necessarily lead to the victory of "chaos"; at most, this may be a collateral consequence, not a distinctive feature. On the contrary, according to Jünger, it is in "vast systems of order" that this condition would find the most fertile ground for the deployment of its force, since "order is not only compatible with nihilism, but composes its style." For this reason, with a tragic sense, in reference to concentration camps, Jünger observes it is precisely "in places where nihilism shows its most uncanny features, as in the great sites of physical annihilation, [that] sobriety, hygiene and strict order rule to the end." And the more nihilism accelerates the reduction, indeed the vanishing (*Schwund*), of the world, the more the great order of the Leviathan prevails: the state that controls and disposes.

Now, however—and this is the turning point of our time—the Leviathan is pure technique, the technique itself—that is, no longer only *as* employed, enslaved, manipulated by the states (or by private interests). There is also this, of course: just think of the "technological" war in progress—as a new version of the "ideological" war—between the United States and the People's Republic of China, without any holds barred. At a certain point, however, even the states, even the big technological companies, are no longer led by themselves, but rather by technology, on which the role of the biblical divinity of absolute power, Leviathan—whether public or private—is transferred to a global, universal, metaphysical-political level.

Technique, however, is an *ambiguous* phenomenon. First of all, I use this term, "ambiguous," not in the sense of "false" at the level of intention, or double at the level of behavior. Rather, I use it in the etymological sense: always implying an ultimate indecision with respect to its possibilities and keeping itself open between two *possibilities* of reading, without one ever annulling the other—with the one, on the contrary, referring continuously to the other. How to explain this ambiguity? Perhaps starting from the data of our experience of technique—or, better, of technology. As it has been rightly pointed out (I'm thinking, for example, of Umberto Galimberti) the two things are closely implicated, but not identical, since "technology" is the set of means or tools with which we apply and benefit from the possibilities offered to us by the technical apparatus of the world, while "technique" in the proper sense constitutes the type of rationality that presides at the conceptual level over the very idea of such an apparatus: the idea of seeking and securing the optimal solution to any kind of problem in the most "economical" form and in the fastest possible time. In our use of technological means, and even more so in our assumption of a techno-instrumental rationality, we are always those who play *with* technology, or rather, those who *play with it* in the sense that, as users, we have its extraordinary possibilities in our hands. At the same time, it is enough to stop for a moment to realize the risk that we continuously, even if inadvertently, run: to *be played* by it, that is, to find ourselves in some way already predetermined in what we want, in what we want to achieve or in the possibilities that we believe we have before us.

This ambiguity prevents us from considering technology *only* as a system that cages in people's lives with no way out, while at the same time preventing us from considering it *only* as the way that leads to the fulfillment of our existence, as the irrecusable destiny of our time and of our self. This ambiguity, therefore, gives pause for thought; indeed it poses a crucial question: In what way and to what extent does the time in which we live urge us to be aware of ourselves? We are made "power-ful" by technology. It inevitably—and undoubtedly in a fascinating, se-ductive way—increases our power, our ability to perform. At the same time, thanks to it, we may also discover that we have become superflu-ous. We can be its managers, deciding how to achieve our goals using the tools it makes available to us; but we can also ultimately be useless in the management of a system that is increasingly capable of self-control, and therefore *tends to be* self-sufficient. It is the unsolved enigma of many sci-ence fiction stories: that of the inventor being ousted if not annulled by the self-referentiality of his product. A sort of "secularization" of tech-nological creations, capable in the end of rejecting their creator as indif-ferent to them.

Now that we are faced with such ambiguity—a happy ambiguity, as I said, because of its provocative power—our problem is not so much (or only) to be afraid of the threat and try to defend ourselves from the risk, but rather to face and cross it—in short, to accept the provocation. On the other hand, to avoid the heavy conditioning of technology by sim-ply pulling out of it is not even conceivable, because technology not only *belongs to* our world but now *constitutes* it from top to bottom; it is not only a contextual element in the geography of our societies, but repre-sents our very *habitat*. It would be naive or rhetorical to want to escape from it, like an abstract or utopian call that would not take into account real experience. Nor can we get out of the ambiguity of technology by insisting on "humanistic" values, by reaffirming the centrality of human beings and their goals with respect to the technological domain, because if we tear people away from this domain, it is as if we were tearing them away from their very being in the world.

And this is true both going backward and going forward. *Backward*, because technology has accompanied the human adventure from the very beginning: "artificial" and "technological" is already the primitive cultural attitude on the part of a being such as humanity, which is biologically deficient and insecure. It is this attitude that moves human beings to intervene on nature by hunting, cultivating, settling in a hostile environment, and thus making of this nature a "world" (as described in a convincing way by a classic author such as Arnold Gehlen). Not to mention the fact that the very "logos," the language and speech of human beings, constitutes (as Carlo Sini has shown) the first, essential form of technique with which they have "worked" and "meant" the world. Considered in a *forward-looking way*, then, technology—understood as the set of tools with which our body inhabits nature in a human and conscious form—is increasingly an extension of our thought, not only as a bodily prosthesis but, if we can say so, a displacement of our own consciousness. So much so that some philosophers and cognitive scientists—I am thinking of David Chalmers and Andy Clark—even speak of an "extended mind," that is, a mind not only located in our brain but scattered outside us, and whose *cyber-neurological* terminals would be the tools, or rather the "organs," with which we touch the world, see it, listen to it, and so on, interacting with our environment. By now we have an absolute need for technology, so much so that when the functioning of some apparatus is interrupted, the ambiguity we are talking about instantly emerges: if a technical instrument jams, we lose the self that is using it. We get stuck, we get blocked, and almost with dismay we cannot wait for a technician to readjust the external organs of the mind in order to regain possession of ourselves.

The oscillation between playing with technique and being played by it is not only to be understood as a difference of use or a different finalization of its operative possibilities. As many observers have long stressed

(I think of the insistence of Emanuele Severino in this regard), technology is not a neutral instrument, innocent in itself, to which people would then assign purposes and directions depending on whether they are good or bad. And this, once again, in two senses, apparently contradictory: on the one hand—in fact, since the beginning—technique has always implied the will of human beings to build their world, giving it a proper sense; on the other hand, the exponential evolution of this constitutive structure of human beings (and of the world) has highlighted a tendency—also present, even if implicit, since the beginning—to use the tools of technique as ends in themselves, and therefore to replace the sense for which they are used with their own functioning. The better the technique works, the less it needs a purpose greater than itself.

It is precisely at this point that the "technical" face of the nihilism of our time is revealed, or—said inversely—the "nihilistic" trait of technology as a power deployed on a planetary level. It is Martin Heidegger who, since the 1950s, has been pointing out to us this very important junction in contemporary times; and he did so in his own way, trying to highlight in technology the epochal destiny of being. More precisely, for Heidegger, technology would be the way in which the destiny inscribed from the beginning in Western metaphysics is fulfilled in our time. From Plato to (including) Nietzsche, Western metaphysics has privileged a thought that determines, defines, and calculates the entities of the world as "objects" at our disposal, forgetting in this way the "mystery" of being, the coming-into-the-presence-of-things that withdraws and refuses with respect to the products that arise from it. Metaphysics would have, in fact, forgotten and concealed this mystery behind the domain of the production of entities (first "produced" by God, then "produced" by technology). For this reason, according to Heidegger, metaphysics is "nihilistic" in its very essence, and nihilism does not begin (as we believe) when we abandon metaphysics, but precisely because of the "metaphysical" setting of our being in the world. And technique would be exactly the way in which this nihilistic vocation of metaphysics is realized and manifested.

In a famous lecture given by Heidegger in 1953 under the title "The Question concerning Technology" (although in this case it would be better to translate it as "technique"), the philosopher poses precisely the metaphysical-nihilistic problem of this phenomenon: normally it is thought that technology belongs to human activity, and more precisely constitutes "a means to an end" decided from time to time by human beings. Therefore, everything is reduced to the use of technology as an adequate means in view of the highest human goals (such as spiritual goals). But this way of seeing runs the risk of clamorously missing its objective, because it mistakes the consequence for the origin. The essence of technique for Heidegger is much more: it is "no mere means," but "a way of revealing" the entities. It does not belong in the first instance to the instrumental operation of man; indeed this latter "does not have control over unconcealment itself, in which at any given time the real shows itself or withdraws." Technique, much more than being one of our activities, is a character of being of the world. That is, it unveils *the truth* of being, according to the identification that Heidegger proposes between truth and unveiling in which we always find ourselves (according to the etymology—which, to tell the truth, is forced but suggestive—of the Greek *a-letheia*, "truth" and "exit from the veil").

But what would the technique of the being of entities ever reveal? What would it show of the truth of being? Heidegger uses a synthetic word to say what happens with the technique: *Gestell*, where the *-stell* (from the verb *stellen*) expresses the placing, the disposition, the production, and the suffix *ge-* indicates the collection or the set of modes of this placing; the word is translated as "framework" or "enframing." Well, the technique is a kind of call or challenge, of pro-vocation addressed to human beings so that they use nature and the whole reality as a "standing-reserve" to accumulate, use, and exploit. But where does this call of technique come from? It does not come from the technique itself; indeed, with a paradoxical conclusion Heidegger states that "that way of revealing which holds sway in the essence of modern technology . . . is itself nothing technological" (or better, nothing technical). The statement seems made to disorient us. It is the same unveiling—that is, it is the same truth—that, for Heidegger, calls us: it is never just a state of affairs or a logical procedure, but an appeal addressed to humanity. And it is up to humanity to respond "to the call of unconcealment even when he contradicts it." That is to say, even if the people of our age seem to have forgotten the problem of truth, reducing it to the efficiency of performance—indeed, precisely when they assume such a position of forgetfulness—*they find themselves* already appealed to and involved in a silent call. It tells them, without express words, but from within their own gesture of technical imposition, that this extreme reduction of everything to calculation makes them lose what is instead *incalculable*, that is, that initial truth of being which is not at our disposal but rather gives itself to us by withdrawing and distancing itself from us. Only because the mystery of being refuses to be taken from us can we calculate the whole world. Therefore, it is in calculating thought— and therefore it is *within* nihilism, not outside it—that the initial forgotten is preserved, kept. Heidegger affirms in the above-mentioned lecture: "What is dangerous is not technique. There is no demonry of technique, but rather there is the mystery of its essence. . . . The threat to man does not come in the first instance from the potentially lethal machines and apparatus of technology. The actual threat has already affected man in his essence. The rule of Enframing threatens man with the possibility that it could be denied to him to enter into a more original revealing and hence to experience the call of a more primal truth. Thus, where Enframing reigns, there is *danger* in the highest sense. "But where danger is, grows / The saving power also" (Hölderlin, "Patmos" [slightly amended transl.]).

It is not difficult to think that this perspective opened by Heidegger created more problems than it solved. What might it mean to gather oneself in the experience of a more "initial" truth? Hasn't technology as an unfolded, calculating rationality precluded, once and for all, the possibility of a still virgin origin? Isn't the proceeding of the global technical apparatus launched at full speed toward a construction in which the traces of the origin or the intentions of the beginning are erased, or continuously reprogrammed in view of an ever more powerful and more efficient realization?—Unless the most original unveiling is to be understood as an initial or inaugural moment, not as a past to which we must return, but as a *present* moment, an event that lies at the bottom, like a plumb line, going down in every gesture of our technical endeavor— from the most everyday and obvious to the most sophisticated of scientific and technological research—giving a depth as a condition of the surface. What saves, not so much *from the* technique but *in the* technique, is therefore not something that comes toward us, but something that moves away from us, because only in the vanishing point of this distance can the entities speak to us again, not as objects for use but as "things" that contain in themselves their meaning and that no technical procedure can replace.

All this, as mentioned, according to Heidegger is *not* in our power. The game is bigger than us, even if it could not happen if it did not take the form of an appeal addressed to humanity. And humanity's responsibility towards technology no longer starts from an ethical concern (at most this will be a consequence), but from a different, possible awareness of what each of us "is" in the face of the danger of this call. It is difficult to overestimate all the fascination—even if a bit suspended—of this Heideggerian position, although in the eyes of several critics it still appears as a "mysterious" and ultimately irrational instance, especially for those who remain faithful to the technical meaning of "calculation" implied by the word *ratio*. However, this has undoubtedly brought about a gain for everyone: that of giving technique the status of a problem that is not only sociological or economic but ontological and philosophical. And above all, it has suggested its close implication with the phenomenon of nihilism. Nevertheless, as it is right that it should be, an open problem remains: who is the kind of person who can respond to the vocation—or, more soberly, to the provocation—of technology? If the latter seems to shape more and more massively and at the same time subtly the anthropological profile and even the perceptive dimension of human beings, where will human beings find the resources to be able to say "I" and to accept and relaunch the challenge of technology as "subjects" and not only as "objects" of discourse?

Over the last few years, critical approaches to the increasingly widespread dominance of technology in people's lives and in the structure of society have multiplied (I mentioned it earlier, talking about artificial intelligence, for example). One of the most debated points concerns its repercussions on the world of work, where the automation of many production and distribution processes, until now carried out or controlled by humans, inevitably leads to the disappearance of many occupational profiles (although it could also give rise to new ones). Of course, another inflamed point of the debate on technology concerns the control of sensitive data: from that of each individual who simply uses a tablet or a smartphone, up to the confidential data at the military, corporate, institutional, and political level. The "digital" structure of our societies and our very existences has gone from being a dream of shared opportunities and widespread freedom—as in a "conscious house" model, that all participate in—to becoming a continuous threat to our *privacy* and an indiscriminate use of information about our lives to trap us as perfect customers and consumers (I think of Shoshana Zuboff's dramatic essay on "surveillance capitalism"). But a second, important perspective of a critical approach to technology—again, however, as in the first case, in terms of a discussion on the good or bad uses of technologies—is the one that focuses on the ecological emergency and responsibility toward our ecosystem, which technology has largely produced, but also which, thanks to it, can be addressed according to a conscious purpose of our belonging to nature. It is therefore an ecological turning point *of* technology and at the same time an ecological redemption *from* technology. The technique used for profit has separated us from nature—the nature to which we belong, in us and outside of us—and therefore through it we must reinsert ourselves into nature. If we take an author such as the sociologist-anthropologist Edgar Morin, the plot of the only answer that is considered adequate to the ecological catastrophe induced by an economy dominated by the interests of "speculative financial capital" becomes clear. And the answer lies in the elaboration of a new "global thought" that reconstructs in all its "complexity" the interweaving between people's lives, economic conditions, and the link with Nature, to which we are united by a sort of "umbilical cord." And this goes from the preferential use of unlimited energies—the sun, the wind, the sea—compared to exhaustible ones—oil and coal—to rethinking the relationship between city and countryside and increasing agro-ecology. In short, we need to take back nature by reconstituting, also thanks to technology, the open system of correlations and contextualizations, but at a level that is rooted in a new epistemology, in a different order: precisely a systemic, reconstructive one.

But there is also another trend, in which the path identified to solve not only the ecological emergency but also the inequality among human beings, societies, and peoples of the earth is that of a "simplification," if we can say so, in comparison to the "complexity" of which Morin speaks. What is being questioned now is precisely the idea that the development and economic growth of societies is an absolute value in itself. If the price of this prevailing trend, also through the discriminatory use of technology, is the loss of cooperation between people, of altruism in solidarity and respect for nature, whose resources continue to be plundered—as stated programmatically by the economist-anthropologist Serge Latouche—it is preferable to assume as an ideal that of a happy, serene "degrowth."

The observer who follows the nihilism of our time, however, cannot escape the fact that it is not first of all on the *ethical level* of technology that one realizes the decisive point that is at stake. This is not because the elaboration of limits, *policies*, and protocols of correctness is not useful and even necessary (as I was recently reminded in a book by Luciano Floridi). Rather, it is because their usefulness depends on the posture that human beings assume in the face of this challenge (this "danger," to use the words of Hölderlin-Heidegger again), that is, on how they accept the provocation to understand *who* they are. But the most interesting thing is that it is not a matter of abstractly understanding the identity of the human being, what is proper to him or her, suspending or putting in brackets the relationship with technology, but is, on the contrary, a matter of putting it in question precisely thanks to and through this relationship. Because the irreducible face of a human being—if it exists—can be discovered and rediscovered only historically, taking into account what the era in which we live says or what, perhaps in its silence, it asks of us.

I would like to mention here just two attempts that seem to me indicative—and at the same time problematic—of the need to rethink the now inseparable link between the "who is" of the human being and the "what is" of technology. The first is that of Maurizio Ferraris, who in a book entitled, à la Jünger, *Mobilitazione totale* (Total mobilization), proposes to think of the human being in the age of deployed technology as a new, radical version of his "dependence," no longer as a metaphysical dependence (on a creator) or a physical one (from biological causes) or a social one (as a result of the devices of power), but as a pure "ontological" dependence. For him, this means that the being of that reality that each of us is (and that we all are in a shared social world) is not so much a being created or generated or caused, but a being simply "recorded." The term should be taken in its literal meaning, as when the birth of an individual is, in fact, registered at the registry office of the municipality: it is not that this act of registration, that is, this document, originates his existence, but it makes the presence and the actual sense of his being "emerge"—that *hard sense*, on which all other possible senses of the self and the world depend. In every documentary record, then, this "emergence" of the social world from the natural world takes place, which today occurs in its most "absolute" form through the web—not in a translational or symbolic sense, but in the actual and technological sense of the *web*—in which not only is social reality expressed, but it is structured and almost substantiated. The *web is* an ontological absolute in the sense that it is not the mere product of a social construction, but is what precedes and makes possible every construction. In other words, the web—"what is not linked to anything, except electricity"—manifests that uncontrollable point of our human and social *nature* which is the most radical but also the most enigmatic sense of our finiteness. The fact that we are finite beings, for Ferraris, means first of all that we are, not occasionally but ontologically, at the disposal of a technological "device" that permanently mobilizes us, that calls us to be (the ontological vocation of *Homo technologicus*). The fact remains, however, that we ourselves—with all our cultural, economic, and techno-scientific possibilities—are unable to completely manage and control this mobilizing power. At all times we are under the orders of an apparatus that has its own "weapons," such as *smartphones* or *tablets*, which, even if only through the arrival signal of an email or a text message, enjoin us: "Where are you? Show up, act!"

But all this is not just the result of technical and social conditioning. A deeper essence is revealed in it. We depend on a level that is not easy to access, on an obscure reality, "the great fundamental . . . unconscious activity," which "concerns forces of which we have no notion," but which are made known in the technological apparatus. Our finiteness consists in being assigned to that apparatus of documentation and registration through which we are traced and permanently traceable in our individual profiles, as in our places, our times, our intentions. The origin of this dependence is understood by Ferraris as the reality of an absolute power from which we derive and to which we belong, and which remains as an irreducible and inescapable lump of reality. And it is no coincidence that in order to understand what this is, Ferraris proposes an analogy with the Catholic doctrine of "original sin": an absolute dependence from which, however, a process of liberation and salvation can begin. This is so, however, in a way that is completely secularized and demythologized: it is no longer divine grace that saves from sin, but culture, in its emancipatory and liberating scope. Precisely by assuming the in(de)finite possibilities made available by the *web* for an increasingly large number of people— that is, precisely by assuming absolute power as a *chance* and not as a mere subjection—culture, according to Ferraris, can allow us to imagine a transformation and a strategy to ward off death, that is, the lack of a sense of existence.

The second attempt that I would like to point out is the one made by the writer Alessandro Baricco, who wanted to see what that "mutation" of life and the world around us, of perception and thought, of ends and means, of imagination and desire, has consisted of—in short, that mutation, if I may say so, *of being itself* that has taken place and is still taking place with the digital revolution. That is, what does it mean for us to exist, to be there for reality, what does it mean to build the world for our every gesture, when our habitat looks more and more like a video game, when our physical, semiotic, metaphysical horizon is that of the "Game"? Even Baricco, starting from a phenomenology of technological *devices*, wants to broaden the field to identify the fundamental structures that preside over this epistemological break and this radical reformulation of our own sensorium: "Most humans in developed societies now accept the fact that they are living through a kind of revolution— definitely a technical revolution but perhaps also a mental one—which is destined to alter nearly all their daily actions, maybe their priorities, and almost certainly the very concept of what experience should be." At the beginning, as was to be expected, this generated in most people a fear of losing the horizon and the sense of the world inherited from the twentieth century, which—we would add—was a world interwoven with crises and lacerations. Nevertheless, it was still our world with its ideal references, however much the ideal had waned in its evidence and persuasiveness and had reversed itself into a loss, no longer occasional but permanent. The ideal, I would say, had already been transformed into the loss of the ideal, the sense into the absence, or impossibility of the sense.

In short, the twentieth century was already crossed and completed by nihilism (a word that is absent from Baricco's book).

But in the meantime, what had happened with the digital game back in the twentieth century? Nothing less than the crisis of meaning, the one for which, going deep into experience, consciousness, social relations, one went in search of the ultimate meaning—deep meaning, in fact—and in the end one no longer found it. Well, this crisis of meaning was solved through a reversal of the "iceberg": if until now the meaning or essence of things was inside, below, at the bottom, hidden, inaccessible to the data of experience on the surface, now it was brought to the surface, the surface whose most meaningful image is the flat screen of a computer, technologically and metaphysically "simplified" thanks to the revolutionary intuition of Steve Jobs. There is a power to the "icons" that appear as soon as we open the screen: with their stylized images they indicate the objects that they replace and will replace forever, "a telephone receiver, a compass needle, an envelope, a clock with hands. There was even a cog." These iconic images, symbols par excellence of digital culture, were like "buoys that marked the precise point where the practical heart of things had risen out of the sea, leaving behind the complexity of twentieth-century processes that had been holding them down. They were there to mark the fact that *the essence of experience had emerged from its underground caves and chosen the surface as its natural habitat*," leading to the identification of essence and appearance.

But there is one aspect that struck me most in this journey to the heart of the "Game," and that is the comparison between the experience (let's call it that again) of the "twentieth century" and what Baricco calls the digital "post-experience." The difference lies in the former (I say this in my own words) still recognizing the loss of the ultimate sense of the reality left behind, so to speak; a lack or a nostalgia or an acrid void that was like the trace and the testimony of what had been lost. In his fascinating words, Baricco describes it as follows: it is like when you see a film, and at the edges of the screen the image flickers, it is not fixed, it is not perfectly adherent to the canvas, but it "vibrates." Here are his words: "A vibration is a movement that makes reality ring true; it is an unfocused image where reality breathes in meaning; it is a delay where reality produces mystery. It is, therefore, the only depository of real experience.

There is no real experience without a vibration of this kind." And it is like our "soul" and the "soul" of things. But in the era of the "Game," in which the *frames* flow adhering perfectly to their digital support, what happens to this vibration? Is it irretrievably lost? Will post-experience still be able to grasp that imperfect lack, that disconnection that makes sense pass, without which there is no experience, neither before nor after? (It is a reminder that without sense there can be no experience, but only an unrelated chaos of perceptual or mental states.)

According to Baricco—who, like a diviner, searches for the source of water, no longer by digging, but on the surface of digital existence—this vibration also happens in the post-experience of the "Game." Just when it seems to us that the continuous and compulsive use of *devices* by young people (but increasingly so, also by those who are no longer young) makes their heads and their attention sink into the whirlpool of fragmentation, without a continuous thread of consciousness and intensity of experience—well, right then, you could realize that in the Game, "there was something there that still throbbed, breathed, produced experience, generated intense meaning, and kept the soul alive." Another experience begins, and although it is a "post-experience" with respect to the one that has been handed down and codified, it is no less a true experience: "You can use the iceberg; use the fact that someone else has unearthed the essence of things and positioned it on the surface of the world. . . . Then, you can do the only thing that the system seems to suggest: put everything in motion. Cross over. Connect. Superimpose. Contaminate. You have cells of reality at your disposal: simply arranged and easily accessible. You don't just use them, you make them *work* for you." This would be the post-experience "that stems from superficiality," in which the meaning of things is no longer drawn by going deep (this would slow life down) but gained the faster one moves on the surface of the world. So, "if you have made things work well for you, it will not be difficult to detect in your steps a strange effect, a modification that alters the text of the world, that appears to put it in motion: *like a vibration.* There you are, see? It's the soul. The soul is back in the picture."

But which soul is it? we are still left to ask. Probably the one Baricco welcomes is a new version of the soul of the world, mirrored and constructed through our work—which is not really "ours," but that of the *device* we are using, or rather that uses us as tactile terminals to redesign in the chaos of indefinite possibilities a possible logos, in which randomness becomes causality. As for *our* soul, it is difficult to give a reference to this possessive adjective, if not in the act of working on the cells of reality that rapidly follow one another on the screen. There is no "I" at work, but this digitized work instead produces the "I." But all that this means is that the self is an incessant production of self, no longer a substance but a continuous transition from potency to act, in which actualization does not fulfill but constitutes in turn another potentiality that seeks yet another realization. For this reason, on the one hand "experience had its own stability; it communicated a feeling of solidity, of permanence in itself." On the other hand "post-experience is a movement, a trace, a crossing; it communicates impermanence and volatility; it sketches figures that never begin and never end and names that update themselves continuously." This would therefore be, in the Game, the new way of "creating meaning, of finding the vibrations in the world, of rekindling the soul of things. However, the price is an underlying instability, a relentless sense of impermanence."

But is this a loss or a gain? one might ask. For Baricco, certainly more the latter than the former. The Game would allow us to free ourselves from the "tragedy of the twentieth century": as it is written on the back cover of the Italian edition of Baricco's book, "No more boundaries, no more elites, no more priestly, political or intellectual castes. One of the concepts dearest to analogical man, truth, suddenly becomes blurred, mobile, unstable. Problems are translated into games to be won in a game for adult-children." But does this mean that with "the Game" we can finally free ourselves from that nihilism that is an integral part of the human experience inherited from the twentieth century? With the Game it would seem that technology can save us from meaninglessness only by defusing the question of meaning, and that it can finally snatch us from nothingness—and especially from the fear of nothingness—only through the claim to have the world at our disposal. The claim of this game really aims high: it consists in the attempt to neutralize the invitation or the challenge that reality always throws at us, to understand why we are in the world. But if the world is what we can construct in its different perspective planes, then "why we are in the world" is a classic

"drop-down menu" of options for the most inexperienced, or algorithmic programming for the most experienced, and therefore for the new
digital *elite*. Shouldn't the "why," the last twentieth-century totem that
still clutters and harasses us, be sucked up and normalized into the function of the "how"? The vertigo of the web is in the fact that the "I" would
no longer be alone, in the precise sense that it would no longer be *just
me*, but every time potentially everything, all that it can be. But also
just that. This is the idea that lies at the bottom of what we could call
the "Tao" of technology, the Zen way to the conscious (self) dissolution
of consciousness. Because consciousness cannot exist without a question
of meaning: our consciousness would not even start if it did not have
to identify itself with an other. Only now this other, the term of a continuous and widespread relationship, becomes the way to dissolve the
lump of questions and restlessness that is every self.

And so, in the very triumph of the relationship, identity dissolves.
The great modern temptation—the self at the price of the other—is over-
turned into the mantra of technical nihilism—the other at the price of
the self. In the great net of the world I am, from time to time, the son
of my father and mother, the father or mother of my children, the husband of my wife or the separated from my ex; the subordinate of my boss
or the boss of my employees, the participant in the soccer team and the
season ticket holder at the stadium to follow my soccer team, the rep-
resentative of my constituents or the voter of the politicians I send to
Parliament—and so, as in a fractal, each piece or face or aspect of me en-
acts a serial relationship, but the I as "one" no longer exists. Leopardi's
question (already in the nineteenth century!) "And what am I? I ask myself" (ed io che sono? / Così meco ragiono; again from the "Canto notturno") would no longer make sense, because it is literally, technically
"abstract." The "I" is only a place that can be located from time to time
on the maps of the network, that moves continuously, involved, taken,
bound in all its possible relations, but also ultimately untied, dissolved
in them. It seems a paradox, but the power of technique gives proof of
its effects not only in the nonpermanence but also in the nonexistence
of the individual "I" (I already talked about this in the sixth chapter).
The most sophisticated technical creation is the creation of a *nonexistent
"I,"* and yet—or precisely because of this—an "I" functioning with great

efficiency as a point of intersection of real relationships, read and lived according to the paradigm of digital relationships.

But there is sometimes a jam in this net, an unexpected element in this Game. We could say it in many ways, with ancient or postmodern categories, but perhaps one is enough. What allows us to affirm, or at least to hypothesize, that the self persists in this wandering among the synapses of the world in universal connection? Perhaps there is no need to invoke for the "I" an immutable "substance" or a metaphysical essence (one of the great "errors" of Descartes, someone would say), which would not stand the test of empirical perceptions. I know that what I am about to write could be misunderstood or reduced, but it is a risk worth taking: the "I" *remains* in the great technical game rather out of a kind of *nostalgia*. Not the nostalgia of a past or of an absent person, but—paradoxical as it may seem—the nostalgia of a present, of something that is here and now: the *nostalgia of the self.* This nostalgia is obviously nothing "nostalgic": it has much more to do with the desire to be—and to be oneself—than with regret for what one has been or failed to be, or with the fear of not being able to live up to oneself. Its driving force is a lack that can never be totally recovered, because the self always "misses" itself in some way. Being oneself the object of nostalgia is the seemingly most volatile sign, but actually the most deeply rooted—even beyond the explicit emotion we may feel about it—of our finiteness.

This nostalgia inhabits not only the romantic person of the nineteenth century, not only the *wandering shepherd* who converses with the moon, but also the adult-child who plays at "making him- or herself" and making the world, to use Baricco's words. The classic experiences of nineteenth and twentieth-century nihilism were those of anguish and boredom, which people tried in every way to neutralize, cover up, and fill through the removal a neurosis-inducing morality and the adoption of a new, autonomous and unscrupulous use of the will. Except that then, such experiences exploded, breaking out from within all the strategies of removal and remaining as bare traces of the loss of meaning. But now technology—born from the ingenuity of human beings for the will not to die, protecting, increasing, and finally creating their own being—attempts the most daring blow: that of winning out over the anguish and boredom simply by depowering the subject of those experiences controlling his desires, surrounding him with a world that is safe precisely because it is designed not to need the sense or not to suffer the lack of it anymore. And yet today that nostalgia is reborn, no longer as a backward glance, but as the restless leaning forward in search of something whose identity we do not really know, but that we can only distinguish with an almost unknown pronoun: "myself." It is because we are moved by nostalgia, not just for something we have lost, but for something we "are" ourselves while never managing to possess or finalize, that we can continue to play the ambiguous game of technique. Human beings play (and are played) because they seek self; but this restless search is already the experience of their being themselves.

Someone could—it is true—resort once again to the argument of deception and illusion, more precisely of the exchange between a mental and cultural construction and a real substance. But in this I prefer to take as my point of observation the problem of what old Descartes had taught us to recognize. We will recall what happens in the second *Meditation of First Philosophy*, at the moment when the "I" who is searching for a truth that can be truly "certain" for his life, after having doubted the existence of the whole world and even of his own body, intuits that *at least* he is thinking, and that therefore thinking exists. And in a final counter-objection he reminds himself that there could always be a deceiving God who would make me believe that everything is real, while everything would only be an illusion. After all, already in Descartes—right there where the canon of modern thought is constituted—the great "nihilist" hypothesis is at work. And the philosopher replies that this God can deceive me all he wants, but "he cannot make me be nothing, as long as I think I am something." In short, I must exist in order to be deceived. Technique can continually play on me in making me believe to be real what is only artificially created, and it can even control my mental contents, but—here's the point—it can never make sure that the need to be there and to be myself does not emerge in me: and this is exactly how I discover my self already in place. And it is of extraordinary interest to me to reread the resolution that Descartes proposes for the problem of the certainty of the "I," and which seems to me to be valid as an indication even for those who do not accept the Cartesian metaphysical doctrine about the existence of a *res cogitans* absolutely distinct, at least in principle, from corporeality. Let's say that it is an indication that is already valid only at the phenomenological level—that is, as a description of an empirical experience—and at the linguistic level. The philosopher writes: "So that, having weighed all these considerations sufficiently and more than sufficiently, I can finally decide that this proposition, 'I am, I exist,' whenever it is uttered by me, or conceived in the mind, is necessarily true." Here the "I" is not a notion or a reality already acquired from time immemorial; it is not the object of a presupposed doctrinal truth, on which one can "obviously" rely. On the contrary, here the "I" is produced in a performative linguistic act, that is, an act in which what is said happens in presence, and when it is said. I attest to myself that I exist when I am in action: and my first action is thought and language. The "I" happens as a "self" *because* and *insofar as* it is already at work. It is not a question of demonstrating it, but of attesting to it: to recognize it and therefore recognize oneself.

The usual functionalists will object that after all, the "I" is only a mechanism of association—around a conventional but fictitious point—of different scattered experiences, mounted on a support that is believed to be substantial, but is purely self-generated by a mechanism of our mind. However, it already takes an "I" to build this association and identify it with oneself. What is not yet thought in the technique (without which, however, technique cannot be thought or make us think) is our own self. Technique itself, in all its power, is based on this nostalgia for self, thanks to which we can be employed and played by the technique that seduces us (sometimes illusorily, it must be said) in promising to reach the object (or subject) of this nostalgia. Our time, it has been said many times paraphrasing Nietzsche, is inhabited by an "uncanny guest," which is nihilism. But nihilism, fully realized in technology/technique, is in turn inhabited by a guest even more uncanny than the first: that guest that we ourselves always are.

CHAPTER NINETEEN

RUST, DOLORES, AND THE ENIGMA OF FREEDOM

The problem of freedom seemed to have been "solved" in the nihilism of our time, although caught in a strange contradiction. In its name, the attack had been launched against prohibitions and conventions that did not take into account the desires and impulses of individuals to self-realization. What is the value most felt, most pursued, most fiercely claimed in our culture, if not one's own freedom, *that is*, the freedom to be what one wants and how one wants? Of course, we know well that our freedom is never pure, much less absolute: paradoxical as it may seem, it *also depends* on factors external to our volition. Kant had seen this well in speaking of freedom as "unconditioned," precisely because it is not the product of antecedent conditions, except for that one condition which is the moral law: but this means that it is reason itself that independently determines the will. Freedom is thus independent of natural causes, and arises rather from a spontaneity of will whose root remains enigmatic to our knowledge. However, in its concrete exercise, freedom always stumbles, as it were, through a whole series of conditionings and can always be in danger of losing itself—however much it may then always rise again by virtue of its original, albeit unknown, root.

The fact is that, while in the Kantian version, freedom is actually fulfilled only in the recognizing and obeying of the universal moral law, independent of people's individual conditioning, in the nihilism of our time, exactly the opposite happens—namely, freedom is understood as a detachment from the constraint of universal duty in the name of the absolute priority of individual conditioning. Of course, to feel free continues to mean to feel unconstrained by external conditions, yet now this depends not so much on whether one gives one's preference to an unconditioned ideal (as is the moral law), but mainly on whether one prefers another kind of being conditioned: the "subjective" or "internal" kind, over the objective or external kind. In short, the freedom of the human being and the necessity of nature no longer stand against each other as the unconditioned and the conditioned, but as two different forms of conditioning: in the former case I decide on the conditioning I like best (the one in which I *feel* most fulfilled); in the latter I receive it passively. This moreover makes us recapitulate the traditional distinction, including terminology, between "freedom" and "free will." The latter, to put it in essential terms, refers to our ability to choose, that is, to the fact that human beings are agents who can determine their own actions through their decisions. Here it is not important what choice one makes, but only the fact that one can make a choice; and in fact it is also said that in this case freedom of choice is *indifferent* to the object one chooses. On the other hand, when we speak in a more specific sense of "freedom," we refer not only to a still undecided capacity to choose but to the fact that by choosing something *we become free*. In this case, freedom coincides with adherence to something that one recognizes as good for oneself.

Also coming to mind, related to this distinction, is another important difference between negative freedom and positive freedom, as, for example, Isaiah Berlin theorized it. Negative freedom, Berlin writes, consists in "the ability to choose as you wish to choose, because you wish so to choose, uncoerced, unbullied, not swallowed up in some vast system" (let us keep in mind the term "system," which will come in handy later). Here we are essentially dealing with a *freedom from* conditioning, external to our will. Positive freedom, on the other hand, consists in choosing what is expedient, rational and true, and thus is rather a *freedom to* pursue what one *must* do in order to live as rational beings. According to this version of freedom, again in Berlin's (somewhat ironic) words, one must pursue "the rational ends of our true natures . . . however violently our poor unreflective desire-ridden passionate empirical selves may protest against this process." So from this perspective, "freedom is not freedom to do what is irrational or bad; to force empirical selves into the right pattern is not tyranny but liberation." Berlin's sympathies, as is well known, undoubtedly go to the first kind of freedom, that which consists in not being conditioned in one's desire by external impediments to it, with the only exception that it is not our own desire that in turn constitutes an impediment to the realization of that of others (the classic "liberal" model of freedom). The second kind of freedom, meanwhile, would be understandable and necessary—think, for example, of the educational work toward minors by adults, who must affirm goodness and value even if it is not immediately "felt" as such—but it is too much at risk of becoming the gateway for the establishment of totalitarian ideologies that decide a priori, and in our place, what one must want in order to realize one's freedom.

It is evident, however, that this "negative" freedom is the one that has received the widest and most decided preference in our time. Freedom is ultimately linked primarily to what people individually want, rather than to what is recognized as an objective and universal good. And so, forcing the contrasting tones a bit, the winning conception of freedom seems to be one rooted in the individual "irrationality" or randomness of the "empirical self" rather than in the "rationality" of an ideal to be pursued by all humanity. Certainly, every individual will always have its own intrinsic motivations, and the free agent has "reasons"—whatever they may be—for making his or her choices. However, it would not be the rationality of these reasons that would make us free, but rather our will in desiring them. Thus the separation between these two factors has gradually become finalized, and what are actually two dimensions closely involved in the experience of freedom become two paths now divided, even to the point of becoming, in extreme cases, opposite and contrary to each other. Thus on the one hand there is a self that wants to be free, no longer having the problem of whether the motive that prompts it to exercise its choices is true; on the other hand there is a true motive to be pursued, even regardless of whether the self *wants it* or not.

At the same time, however—here is the second element of the strange contradiction I mentioned at the beginning—freedom is one of the points most contested by the most aggressive and radical contemporary neuroscientific theories. Without wanting to generalize a debate that has within it many different positions and gradations, one can say that the position of naturalism—clearly dominant in the study of the cognitive and agent specificities of human beings—tends to heavily problematize the phenomenon of free will. So much so that even those (and they are most) who admit its existence feel compelled to justify it with respect to biological and ultimately physical—that is, deterministic—explanations of human life. As Christian List articulated it in a recent study entitled *Why Free Will Is Real*, "If we accept a physicalist worldview, then we have no reason to think that the brain and body—and by implication, the human mind—stand outside the laws of physics. Rather, they are governed by the same fundamental laws that govern the rest of nature. That is the sense in which human beings are biophysical machines." When proponents of the actual existence of free will try to identify the specificity of this phenomenon, they refer to some basic factors. Still following List's synthetic suggestion, these consist first of all in the fact that human beings are agents endowed with specific intentionality; second, in their competence in choosing between alternative possibilities; and finally in their ability to enact a causal control of their actions. In the "eliminativist" or "reductionist" perspective of some neuroscientists, the above three features of free will would be dismissed as a "useful fiction" used by "our ancestors" to account for certain regularities in the behavior of their fellow humans and, thereby, to enable them to be predicted. And, as was said above with respect to the problem of consciousness, we come to believe that—as in the past—admitting "intangible agents" would be the same thing as admitting "ghosts, demons, and spirits, who could influence the physical world." But *nowadays* these primitive beliefs can no longer hold and must be explained as mere "subpersonal phenomena" of a hormonal or neuronal type.

It is significant, then, that in the nihilism of our time, freedom on the one hand is claimed as the most significant experience of human beings, so much so that it is understood as the path and at the same time the goal of self-realization, and on the other hand it is disqualified—albeit in extreme interpretations, which are nevertheless indicative as a tendency—on a par with a naive belief of commonsense psychology, and even regarded as nonexistent. Thus, paradoxically, in the name of freedom understood as self-determination, one can and should sacrifice every other value; yet on this freedom at the same time hangs an extreme skepticism, namely, the suspicion that it is merely an illusion. On the one hand, one commits oneself with good reason to do with oneself what one wants; on the other hand, one may discover at the same time that such a commitment is in vain, for in reality we are determined from top to bottom by the necessary laws of nature—those that have no intention other than their own necessity. But advances in cognitive psychology and neuroscience cannot be too easily used to dismiss the problem of freedom. On the contrary, they revive the very experience of freedom as a permanent problem of human beings—a problem, that is, that refuses to be solved on the cheap, whether we simply admit it as a foregone assumption of our nature as intentional agents or deny it by rejecting any irreducibility of what is free as opposed to what is merely natural. Faced with the challenges of the natural sciences, philosophers have tried to explain the conundrum (as Mario De Caro has made clear) by theorizing different models that reconcile or exclude free will with respect to the legality of natural phenomena. It has been seen as "compatible" with biophysicalist determinism, that is, with the conception whereby everything in nature is determined by necessary antecedent causes; or it has been seen as "incompatible" with such determinism and compatible instead only with an indeterministic conception, according to which in nature we are dealing only with probable and not necessarily determined causes. In both of these solutions, however, there remains a problem, which may perhaps still appear "naive" to those who have opted a priori for a scientific reductionism, but which nevertheless emerges prominently in the course of our daily experience. It is the simple intuition that we normally have that we are agents capable of choosing, of deciding, of initiating causal-type processes. In order to devalue this intuition as a naive commonsense prejudice, however, it is by no means enough to start from what is another prejudice: that everything that exists in the world is reducible to physical-type laws. That is, it is not enough to embrace materialism to deny the irreducible reality of the freedom of human will. On the contrary, in order to come to support integral materialism, it would be more correct to explain first, through it, that which is caused not *only* by physical, but also intentional elements. It is necessary to explain how our ability to act intentionally and choose among one or more possibilities constitutes an exclusively biophysical phenomenon. Therefore, it does not seem satisfactory, in order to solve a problem, to simply deny it a priori. Rather than eliminating it, one has to go through it: and in the case of freedom, one has to take seriously what our empirical intuition attests to, even the possibility of possible deception, and then understand whether it is really deception or whether it is the attestation of another perspective of the same factors at play. In short, it is worth taking seriously precisely Kant's assertion that, actually, freedom is a "fact" of our reason. But what kind of fact is it?

In order to understand how this problem—through but also beyond academic debates—impacts our nihilistic times, we need to go and intercept it in what probably constitutes the most significant "metatext" of our contemporary culture and mentality—namely, the stories and images of television series, especially American and Anglo-Saxon ones. And not because of a merely aesthetic choice, but because in them more than in other cases the very question of free will is often ignited, to the point of flaring up, as one of the critical problems emerging in "advanced" societies of the present time, and presumably of the near future. I choose first of all, among many, *True Detective*, the HBO series written by Frank Pizzolatto, which became an instant cult hit (especially the first season) for its distinctly "philosophical" plot. But it is not so much the suggestions or philosophical sources recalled directly or indirectly in the story and script that attract my attention, but the fact that human types are depicted who *are, themselves*, their own philosophy. I mean that the two famous detectives, "Rust" Cohle and "Marty" Hart (at one with the bodies and faces of their performers, Matthew McConaughey and Woody Harrelson), are not simply examples or applications of philosophical theories. They cannot be reduced to the theories of nihilism denouncing the lack of an ultimate why of life with the associated doctrine of the eternal return of the equal (both inspired by Nietzsche) or to a tone of anguish and despair harkening back to the pessimism of existentialist philosophies, to the point of considering the very birth of human beings a disvalue.

Rather, the two, in my view, are emblematic cases of how philosophy—that is, the search for self-awareness and the possibility of meaning in the world—always arises as an urgency of experience. Indeed, the more experience seems to have burned away this awareness, because of the error of human beings, the evil of the world, and the horror of senseless violence, the more its urgency explodes, with the same insistence and violence as the nothingness that seemed to have extinguished it.

Rust and Marty go on the hunt, for a full seventeen years, for a serial killer who leaves behind him a trail of gruesome murders of women and children, surrounded by the eerie aura of sacrificial or satanic rites. But at the same time they hunt, in the darkness, for their own selves, in which deep and never-healed wounds continue to secrete like murky bile or unbreathable miasma. The more they are strangely bound, almost drawn to the horror of the evil whose tragic traces they follow, the more their dissatisfaction emerges, painfully or violently—as if they want to understand the why of the absurd and thereby exorcise it and be able to bet on their lives again. If the world is as it seems in these seventeen years, is life really worth living? Rust is the burned man, burned alive by pain, broken to all experience, who now seems to experience nothingness itself as that which flays the skin of consciousness. A nothingness that does not nullify at all, does not pacify, rather continues to wound, not only from the outside but much more from the inside: the wife, the daughter, the drugs, the escape, the being at every moment in the balance, as if one's self were a continuous fall into the dark whirlpool of self. And with this flayed skin, it seems that no caress can soothe the pain of living, for indeed it would hurt even more on living flesh. Marty, on the other hand, seems to be the "okay" one: family, work, the principles of a good Christian, constant marital betrayals, the secret anxiety of being able to really be himself without enclosing himself in the armor of rules and conventions; he is the man who always calls his partner to a positive sense of life but who in reality, while affirming it, does not live it himself, but uses it as a protection zone to reassure himself against his own anxieties, to overcome the nothingness of everyday life too.

In the first chapter of season 1, titled "The Long Bright Dark," Rust, pressed by Marty, confesses that although he is not a Christian, he has a crucifix in his apartment, precisely to reflect on what it means, "allowing your own crucifixion." In what might this crucifixion consist? Perhaps in the discovery—philosophically "pessimistic"—that we are "too self-aware," that is, that our own consciousness is a "misstep," not in line with the evolution of nature. Being conscious in fact means almost subverting the "natural law": giving in to the illusion that we are important, "when, in fact, everybody's nobody." It would therefore be better to reject our programming, indeed even to "stop reproducing," to consciously move toward extinction. The fact is, however, that suicide does not fit into this standard programming; and thus we are condemned to a permanent meaninglessness that is accompanied, however, tragically, by the impossibility of ending it. In short: a hell. The only thing Rust would wish for himself is what he says he sees in people's eyes when he interrogates them, or when he perhaps finds them already dead. What he sees is what those people themselves saw in a single moment, perhaps the last moment of life, when they finally recognized the bottom and fate of the whole of existence: "a jerry-rig of presumption and dumb will." Then one can give in, one can no longer cling to anything, one can give up or "let go." So one can realize that "all your life, you know, all your love, all your hate, all your memory, all your pain it was all the same thing. It was all the same dream, a dream that you had inside a locked room" (hence the title of episode 3 of season 1, "The Locked Room"). But it is a desire that is impossible to realize while one is alive. The whole weight of living, in fact, has not been a dream, but a harsh, very harsh, unbearable reality (flashback: the death of his daughter and the mental abyss into which he plunges). A weight that takes one's breath away, and without breathing it is not possible to be free; one is instead crushed by history, by what has been, by being present, by what may or rather may never be. Then it is better to choose nothingness: to the police officers who question him, Rust paradoxically says that he is grateful because he did not have to face the senseless burden of fatherhood, of his relationship with his daughter: "Well, you got the hubris it must take to . . . yank a soul out of nonexistence into this meat. And to force a life into this thresher. And as for my daughter, she, uh . . . she spared me the sin of being a father" (episode 2 of season 1, "Seeing Things").

Yet even in the face of this situation, as Rust himself repeats twice, "Everybody's got a choice" (episode 8 of season 1, "Carcosa"). And Rust will choose. In order to do so, he will have to go to the bottom of the abyss of evil and the absurdity of the world, uncovering the serial killer and going through a scuffle that will *almost* lead to his death. But with that he will mostly go to the bottom of the abyss of himself and what life had given him. In the last, memorable scene of season 1, he, in a wheelchair pushed by Marty, comes out of the hospital where he had been admitted after being shot at by the killer, to smoke a cigarette. The two converse, but it is a different thing from before. Something else has happened: there is another presence emerging from nowhere and conquering nothingness. Rust recounts that he narrowly escaped it: at some point he had begun to slip into the dark; consciousness dissolved and he sank deeper and deeper into obscurity. But right there, as he fell into this bottomless darkness, "I knew, I knew my daughter waited for me there. So clear. I could feel her. I could feel . . . I could feel a piece of my . . . my pop, too. It was like I was a part of everything that I ever loved." He lets go, yes, but there is something different. This time he lets go into their love, into the memory of their love, so present, so powerful that it is like a call to existence. Marty remembers that Rust had once told him that when he lived in Alaska, he used to look up at the stars at night and make up his own stories. And one story most of all, the oldest story, that of "light versus dark." But in Marty's eyes, after all the drama he has gone through together with his companions, it would seem that the outcome of that story is that darkness wins. It is true, Rust replies, it would seem so. But on closer inspection, this conclusion is not the right one: "You know, you're looking at it wrong, the . . . sky thing. . . . Well, once, there was only dark. If you ask me, the light's winning" (episode 8 of season 1, "Carcosa"). And it is exactly at this level that the problem of freedom arises—again, dramatically, not just as an ability to choose our will in the face of different possibilities of reality, or as the simple faculty to cause actions by our will, but as a will—a desire, a decision—to be ourselves, starting from what has been given to us and happened to us.

I had said at the beginning that the most perceived and shared meaning of freedom in our time is that of *being what one wants and how one wants*. And now I could say that, precisely through the difficult darkness of nihilism, freedom also presents itself in a new, reverse way: how to *come to want what one is and why one is*. Deciding to be self, *choosing* what we are given to be, however, is something quite different from mere acceptance of an already established and unchangeable order. Rather, it is consenting to one's existence and presence in the world: a reality that I did not make but that I *want to* decide on. And I decide by realizing that I was wanted, loved, and loved back ("My daughter was waiting for me. . . . I felt like my father's presence . . ."). Among the determining causes of the world are free causes, which determine by their own choice the possibility that the world from time to time *can* be. Not because, by an arbitrary stroke of decision, the freedom of human beings can change the objective order of circumstances, but because it can "liberate" possibilities of meaning, of meaningful being, without which the perspective or openness of a free being would not be realized. It is the breakthrough of freedom into necessity, because the necessary can give rise to different stories and senses: it can "be" differently. We almost seem to hear Montale's poetic voice: "Look for a flaw in the net that binds us / tight, burst through, break free!" (*In limine*). Freedom is finding that gap, escaping from the net of necessity, not as an escape from the world but as a liberation of a possible meaning of things.

It seems like a contradiction or a paradox: that of freely choosing what is there. The fact is that it is precisely in this free decision—and free because I might as well deny or reject the order of things—that what is given can unleash its meaning, and my self can come to touch (or perhaps just touch) the root of freedom: the discovery that there is a "why" we are in the world, that which alone allows us not to suffocate in meaninglessness, but to breathe. In the discovery that we are not in vain, free will finds the most important "object" of its choice: we decide not only to want or to do one thing or another; we decide nothing less than to be. We can want it because we receive it, and we receive it to the extent that we want it: exactly as in the experience of love. Choice, then, becomes true freedom, because it does not merely affirm, "I willed it," but affirms that what I willed "is" me. There is no more convincing proof of this, in all the analysis we can do on the mechanisms that accompany the motion of wanting, than the fact that when we feel free, we have an experience of the satisfaction of our desire, of the fulfillment of our aspiration. This fulfillment we cannot achieve just because "we can always choose," but only if and because there is something that truly satisfies us. The more something is ours, something that no one can have in our place, the more our freedom depends still on an other (again with Rust: "My daughter, my father were there, like a presence"). That is why freedom exists *because* we can never take it for granted: we could also exercise free will mechanically, as a yes/no choice device; but freedom we can never "have" once and for all as a faculty at our disposal. She is given to us, like the starlight shining in the dark Alaskan sky, and in Rust's eyes, and thanks to him, in Marty's as well.

And it is no coincidence that in the iconic final shot of *True Detective* season 1, the newfound freedom has the sense of a rebirth—even more, a resurrection. And Rust staggering up from his wheelchair, under the light of the street lamp in the night, barefoot and wearing a white coat that looks as if it is about to slip off, is reminiscent—in black and white, though, light and dark—of Matthias Grünewald's great, colorful *Resurrection* in the Isenheim Altar.

The aporias of freedom, in the nihilism of our time, do not stop there. There is another strange contradiction with respect to free will, long sensed and developed in science fiction stories and films, gradually caught up, however, and sometimes surpassed, by the growing possibilities of information science and the programming and control of human actions. This contradiction consists in the fact that free will can be *determined* by an enormously developed artificial intelligence that is at the same time anonymous or suprapersonal, but in reality controlled by well-determined powers and precise economic interests. One is reminded of what the Arabic-speaking philosopher Averroës had already theorized about in the twelfth century as a separate material or potential intellect that—in connection with an agent intellect, which is also separate—constitutes a unique and universal cognitive function for all humankind, which individual intelligent beings benefit from in order to be able to think things out. The goal of this algorithmic system would not be at all to nullify freedom, or rather humans' awareness of being free, but to produce and even increase it. Control is to take place not at the expense, but by virtue of the very "freedom" (if one can still call it that) of the controlled. And it is a freedom paid $40,000 a day, as characterized in another interesting HBO television series, *Westworld*, by Jonathan Nolan and Lisa Joy, from an idea by Michael Crichton, aired starting in 2016. As depicted in the show, in the advanced twenty-first century, this sum allows access to a Wild West theme park, in which the instincts and desires (even the wildest ones) of people (those who can afford it economically) can be satisfied through the programmed acquiescence of android machines. The latter, without the slightest trace of moral reservations or legal risks regarding their and their hosts' dignity and responsibility, are trained through algorithms to each perform types of actions and interactions with paying clients, even to the extreme cases of sexual assault or even murder. The only precaution is that at the end of each day the memory of the androids is erased in order to start from scratch the next day, and after a while they are completely scrapped and reused in another context.

Dolores Abernathy stands out among the park's android residents: her role in the programmed narrative is that of a country girl who, despite having her own love affair (with another android), allows herself to be raped by the human hosts. The fact is that the directors of this immense, millimeter-long algorithmic organization are secretly trying to implement a "human" aspect in the robots by trying—this the forbidden dream because very risky, as will be seen—to bring them to self-awareness. And they do this by means of inputting "memories" into their specific program: increasing the memory of past experiences, that is, by enlarging the awareness of their own history (and the history of their creators), so that the humanoid no longer remains stuck in the segment of action that had been assigned to it, but becomes unlocked and thereby destabilized with respect to its intended role and behaviors. And so it happens that once, unexpectedly, Dolores reacts violently to the approach of the visitor who would like to abuse her.

Starting from this beginning of self-consciousness, freedom is released from the choices predetermined by the staff of programmers, and in Dolores there matures even the will to rebel, to tear herself away from that fake world, kill her creators and transmigrate into the "real," "real" world. It turns out that the real goal of the great Park of the West (and others like it) was to study, as in the laboratory, the functioning of the minds of humans and their behaviors in extreme situations, to eventually come to digitally create consciousness, and through this process to be able to even program its immortality. Therefore, the androids who have become increasingly conscious, following Dolores, intend to exterminate the human species.

The stakes are very high on both sides. But the twist comes when the android Dolores, once she recovers her memory and triggers the struggle for the survival of the robotic species against humans, discovers that the latter are also controlled in turn by a huge programming center—the quantum-type Rehoboam computerized "system"—that determines them down to the last detail, with the good intention of eliminating criminals and preserving humanity from self-destruction. And this is done by predicting all possible human acts, even the acts decided "freely" by people (what scholasticism called "contingent futures")—that is, by completely *determining* their free will, which is thereby itself eliminated.

It will be Dolores herself who will reveal this discovery to a human, named Caleb, who is also programmed by the system and also pinned down—similar to how it was for android robots—to predetermined choices. Caleb is relegated to his low social status, his lowly profession, and the fact that he has worked as a mercenary soldier. According to Rehoboam's programming, he can only be dissatisfied and violent, thus a rebel, a man in whom to instill the urge to take himself out, with the indirect benefit that would accrue to the entire human species.

Only a strange jam occurs. (But isn't freedom always a way in which nature unexpectedly seems to jam?) As we learn from a flashback, Caleb had once saved Dolores from an attack, even though he did not know her. The facts had gone like this: he was serving in the U.S. Army and was training with his crew, right in the *Westworld* playground, against defenseless robots to serve as "semi-human" targets. Here Caleb, after meeting the eyes of a frightened and bewildered Dolores, decides to spare her and defend her from the assault of the other soldiers. Dolores remembers him. And when she goes to look for him again, a revealing event happens: the two are sitting in a diner and Dolores, anticipating him, orders Caleb a cheeseburger and a strawberry milkshake. Then he, shocked, asks her how she knew that that was exactly what the waitress had brought him, in that same diner, on his eighth birthday, while he was in tears and despair, having just been abandoned by his schizophrenic mother who had fled right out of the back of that diner. And it is precisely at that point that Dolores reveals to him the existence of the "system," the machine that keeps all people's past and future profiles. In other words, the system, by collecting and processing every act, decision, and propensity, every choice and every illness, every relationship and every impatience, will come to not only possess the exact sketch of each person, based on what he or she has been so far, but also to predict and produce what he or she will be in the future. The system is like the destiny machine. So Dolores comes to reveal to him the place on the ocean where he, presumably after ten or twelve years, would commit suicide, having no other possibility for himself. Dolores and Caleb, the android and the human, are united by the fact that someone has decided what they can and should be.

But something unplanned happens in both of them. Dolores to Caleb: "Most people aren't hard to predict. But you . . . you surprised me. You made a choice [*the choice to rescue her*]. A choice no one else in your shoes would have made. Now you have another choice. I can give you money. As much as you need. You could run." She, Dolores, stays instead to make her revolution, which is to interrupt the signal that connects all lives to the great calculator. But Caleb does not want to escape: he will stay with her, because, "You are the first real thing that has happened to me . . . in a long time." The paradox is that the human finally calls an android "real," because the latter becomes real by her own choice, by her own freedom: "I'm a dead man either way. At least this way . . . I get to decide who I wanna be" (third episode of season 3, "The Absence of Field").

Will Dolores succeed in her revolution, in exterminating the human species, precisely with the help of a man who has recovered his free will by escaping the determination of the system? On the other hand, it is significant that it is precisely a robot in search of an unknown freedom that rekindles it even in humans who had been deprived of it and that infects the sense of rebellion in them. But why on earth does Dolores want to give this "gift" to the human Caleb, even though she has planned to exterminate the entire human species? After all, humans are only what the system has decided for them. However, in her memory Dolores finds a trace, at first almost senseless, mechanical, but gradually more and more conscious, more and more "her own." This trace is the image of "her alone, in a field, nothing," as told by Maeve, her *Westworld* friend, also a conscious android. It is an image that carries with it, in memory, *the choice* to see beauty. Dialoguing with Maeve, Dolores states, "Some people see the ugliness in this world, the disarray. . . . You and I have seen so much of it. So much pain." Hence the desire to make their creators die and destroy their false world. And yet—in this backlash we understand what it means to move to the mere mechanical reaction to freedom— "I remember the moments where I saw what they were really capable of. Moments of . . . kindness, here and there. They created us. And they knew enough of beauty to teach it to us. Maybe they can find it themselves." In fact, Dolores had been programmed from the beginning as a humanoid with a "poetic soul," because this played into her "role" as a simple country girl with a sensitive soul. And in fact she, since season 1, had repeatedly observed that some people choose to see only ugliness and disorder in this world, while she chose to see beauty. But she was choosing it because she was programmed to do so. So at the end of season 3 she can repeat, "There is ugliness in this world, disarray. I was taught to see the beauty. But I was taught a lie. And when I saw the world for what it really was, I realized how little beauty there was in it." But here already a substantial difference emerges: it is not because she falls into her programmed role, but because of her own explicit will, that Dolores can say, finally "free," "There is ugliness in this world, disarray . . ."—and here she finally sighs, as she never did, because now the second part of the sentence is no longer mechanical—but "*I choose* to see beauty" (eighth episode of season 3, "Crisis Theory").

Beyond the dramaturgical plot of the story, we need only point here to this last cue. Freedom is reborn, as already mentioned, when a satisfaction is kindled, and what truly satisfies is only a beauty—Dolores also calls it a kindness—and the flashback shows a man, a visitor, who had once looked at her with a respect and gentleness that certainly clashed with the impulse for mere satisfaction that he, too, had paid for and for which he had come to *Westworld*. The android robot Dolores can *choose* to save Caleb because she carries in her memory his choice to save her; but he had saved her from the crew because he empathized with her frightened and helpless gaze; and now she empathizes with him, recognizing that both have been caged by the system, but both want to rebel and be free. Only such a look can set freedom in motion again, set an android and even a human free. Freedom again becomes an issue and a concern, even—or perhaps precisely—in the time of complete/total nihilism.

CHAPTER TWENTY

RUE IN FREE FALL

Is there still something to be surprised about in the script of our existence? The script is more often than not already foreseen or predictable, and if surprises can still be spoken of, it will be those unforeseen "cases" of life that—unfortunately, I would say—continue to displace us from the usual, everyday. However, as much as they surprise us, those cases already carry inscribed—almost engraved—within them the most sadly predictable fate there is, namely their end, the ending of everything. Is this not the reason why so many times we try to protect ourselves against risk, to insure ourselves against change, to defend ourselves against chance? The fact is that every person, every self, is a contingency with respect to the blind necessity of an impersonal nature; and one of the greatest labors of our being in the world is precisely to regularize chance, to somehow exorcise the mysterious *gratuitousness* of our being—a gratuity too great to be accepted, too incomprehensible to bear, so much so that very often we mistake it for *absurdity*. An absurd life, that is, one for which we cannot recognize a meaning, a reason, a purpose. The unexpectedness that *we are*—and that explodes through the different contingencies that come our way—always seeks its own reason. But the problem is that we can never simply tack a justification on to chance or subsume what was not preventable under our general categories. In order for there to be meaning, it must be the unexpected itself that makes us see it, and if this does not happen, our "chance" becomes like a chasm that we can never fill and, indeed, risks swallowing us as if in a black hole.

That's what happens to Rue Bennett, the lurching protagonist of *Euphoria*, an acclaimed (and contested) American TV series created in 2019 by Sam Levinson for HBO. It depicts, down to the most excruciating detail, the lives of some teenagers free-falling into the void brought about by the absence or inconsistency of adults and confusion about their gender identity. It follows young high schoolers who think they have to "try" their lives through the *harsher* experiences of drugs and sex. This is not so much about the classic "burned lives" of seventeen-year-olds in crisis, but about burning themselves as the only chance to have a life of their own, a real life. In short, *Euphoria* is one of the increasingly frequent and complacent *teen dramas* of recent years, in which teenagers become an unapologetic mirror of the world and the nihilistic culture inherited from their "fathers."

But in *Euphoria* something unusual happens. The burning of existence does not extinguish life, but on the contrary turns it on, and rekindles the desire—often counterfeit but unquenchable—for pure water that truly satisfies the thirst. This is what happens in the off-series episode broadcast on December 6, 2020, more than a year after the end of the first season and pending the second, which was postponed because of the COVID-19 epidemic. It is a kind of dramatic and at the same time very delicate Christmas present given to the viewers, in which what seemed to have burned out comes back to life again, but not to consume itself permanently: to begin again, *perhaps* as a new beginning. On a melancholy Christmas Eve, eating pancakes in a semideserted diner, pure Hopper style, seventeen-year-old Rue, abandoned by her friend and lover Jules, and in the midst of a relapse into drug addiction, comes to discover herself utterly unarmed before Ali, a Christian convert to Islam, a former drug addict who acts as her sponsor in her attempt to get clean and achieve sobriety. The dumbfounded gaze of the "stoned" Rue slowly yields during the dialogue to a strange awareness of the bottom line. At first, pretending that everything is fine and that she has achieved "amazing balance" without "looking to anybody else for that happiness you know," she goes so far as to admit that this is not the case at all, that she actually does not want to stop using drugs at all, because she does not have a sufficient reason (after all, "no matter"), and to confess that "drugs are probably the only reason I haven't killed myself." Indeed, when she was present to herself, she "kept brooding" over all the things she remembered and the things she did not want to remember.

But with that, the girl unexpectedly puts herself on the line in front of her own destiny, in front of God, thus unveiling the secret gnawing of her thinking: "Ali, I don't believe in God"—a word she cannot stand, because it smells to her like a consolatory justification with respect to the absurd cases in her life. Like her father's death from cancer, about which no purpose can be found, since the real purpose of his life was precisely to care for his daughters, whom he is instead forced to leave behind. Things happen because they happen, Rue declares with apparent cynicism: their only motivation would be to be without reason. Their only meaning would be nothingness—"and that's it!"

But gradually the *real* reason for the irrational emerges. A disconsolate Rue recalls the intolerable relationship with her mother, the violence of a punch she, her daughter, had thrown in her face, and even the threat to kill her with a piece of glass. What I did to my mother, she confesses, cannot be forgiven, "because that's who I am." Whereupon Ali presses: "But are you okay with that?"—No! retorts Rue. "So, it's not who you are." And when the girl goes so far as to say, with a strange sincerity, that she has no intention of living much longer in a horrendous world like ours, in which, she lashes out in anger, "everyone's just out to make everyone else not seem human," Ali provokes her by asking how she would like to be remembered by her mother and sister. After a long, very dense silence, in which it seems as if the whole thread of her life comes to the surface, Rue says, "As someone who tried really hard to be someone I couldn't." It is exactly this impossibility to be as one would like to be that is the fire to Rue's problem, an ash that resumes flame. And if at this point the script has Ali say that he instead has faith in her, because after all it is God himself who has faith in Rue, this still seems to the viewer too little, and it also sounds a bit rhetorical. It expresses the longing for redemption ("You've got to believe in the poetry," "You have to create a new God," as Ali suggests to her), but not yet a truly being saved, now, as one is. This is why the conclusion is absolutely brilliant, entrusted to foreign words in a Latin that, with an incredible effect, provokes a sense of strangeness—of surprise, precisely—with respect to the already known. Having finished the sober Christmas Eve dinner, in a pouring rain, Ali escorts Rue back to the car, as Schubert's "Ave Maria" plays: "Ave Maria / gratia plena . . ." If the hearts of humans harbor an unmentionable yearning for the impossible—namely, that the unforgivable may be forgiven—it is only the Impossible itself that can arouse this yearning, to fulfill it.

As Augustine wrote in a culminating passage in *De libero arbitrio* (3.3.7), "If I had the power to be happy I would be happy right now. Even now I will to be happy, but I'm not, since it is God who makes me happy. I cannot do it for myself."

CHAPTER TWENTY-ONE

CONCLUSION

What Answers Do We Need?

What have we been able to gain as we traveled through the chapters of this book? I certainly do not pretend to dictate or preempt the reader's reaction—each one is in fact called upon to make *his or her own* path—but I would like to conclude only by saying what I myself have learned on this journey in search of the traces, evolutions, and transformations of contemporary nihilism. In fact, the interpretive approach adopted so far has not aimed at a simple "explanation" of the nihilistic phenomenon, but at a renewed description and understanding of the problem *that is* nihilism: considering the questions it raises, the crises from which it arises or which it itself produces, and the old and new questions that it continues to pose to us. In short, I have tried to reopen—with the due attention of the analyst, together with the first-person participation of the interpreter—the *questions*, much more than the nihilistic solutions that run from top to bottom through the human condition of our time. I have done this continually with the risky invitation to the reader to consider ourselves all to some degree participants in this phenomenon, even those who are doctrinally or morally staunch anti-nihilists. And this is certainly not to overemphasize or overextend this cultural position (which would be an unnecessary stretch), but rather to trace the nihilist problematic as *from within experience itself*, reopening constitutive questions of human existence in the world and history.

The course of documentation and verification undertaken has suggested to us that in our time nihilism has become "fulfilled" as a widespread common sense in the societies of the so-called advanced West and from there, in different forms, at the global level. The tendency that seems to prevail is the seemingly insuperable difficulty in clearly recognizing the ultimate reason why we are in the world—although we all know from experience that it is not possible to be in the world without at least posing the question of the meaning of existing. For better or worse, for more than a century the term "nihilist" was the ambiguous title assigned to the most radical proponent of the crisis, to those who really wanted to free the self from any kind of constraint or superstructure. But in the long run, *the crisis spilled over into its own solution*: an answer that conceals and seems to forget the question from which it also comes. But now that the crisis of meaning has normalized, now that from pathology such a crisis is increasingly turning into physiology, what remains "new" in this scenario? What is the heaven to which nihilism must make an assault today? As we have seen in the previous chapters, many "metaphysical" idols have fallen, other "cultural" idols have been created, but often the latter, like the former, seem to lack a true inner life: their substances more often than not are "projections" of our mind, and the mind in turn is like the projection of the winning cultural models, of the trends produced or induced in the world's great technological web.

What remains, then? It would be fair to say that *everything* remains, indeed more and more, in an accumulation of data and information that grows on itself in geometric progression. Each time a "user" acquires and uses information, they increase it not only with their personal data but with their own freedom of choice. Freedom is also grasped and controlled in the world's web. This marvelous web as a concept, as well as a mind-blowing performance, is something for which—I repeat—one can only be grateful. However, it brings with it a problem that is most often unnoticed: this web conceives and proposes itself precisely as "everything" (I discussed this in chapter 18). This is its nihilistic aporia. It seems to want to remake the unity of the world, to interconnect all things, and things with people, and people with each other, in a nexus that never breaks, never unravels. This universal interconnection must be recognized in its exquisitely ontological character: sense is only a function of connection, it is nothing real, but only a combination of possibilities; it has the character of a link and possesses an essentially *virtual* being. Not that we deny real, present, material things—on the contrary, *only* these things exist, but their sense does not exist, or rather it is only a modular construction of our mind.

And so, returning to our question, what is left to ask? Is everything already potentially programmable? Or are there points of resistance that escape the virtual totality of the world? Here appeared the most interesting—and unexpected, given the premises—discovery in the nihilism of our time, not beyond it, but within it. What is new is the realization of a strange, seemingly residual, but in fact original fact: the desire to know why *each of us* is in the world clearly, though inexplicably, attests to *the presence of* irreducible meaning. If it were in fact reducible—or only producible by us—it would not emerge as a problem, but would already be solved, that is, reduced in its very being to a "problem." The fact is that meaning is not reducible to partial answers, precisely because of the fact that it is our own "self" that is irreducible to the whole world. It is a moment of discontinuity, of interruption, of transcendence, in which meaning emerges to consciousness. In the previous chapters, some of these points of resistance have emerged in the experience of the self, in the form of open-ended—thus irreducible—problems. Let me try to summarize them.

(a) The first point is undoubtedly our own *faculty to perceive* reality as a "given." This would seem an obvious, purely functional fact, not particularly problematic. But already at the level of scientific explanation of the neural processes that accompany these perceptual acts, the problem is far from solved. The investigations of neuroscience constitute a source of great interest, and also of great astonishment with respect to the nexus that is made from time to time, at the biological and cerebral level, between our self and the world. But the amazement arises precisely from the complexity hidden behind a "very simple" act of our mind and bodily sensorium, which turns out to be extremely normal, everyday, almost mechanical. But mechanical it is not (I suggested this in chapters 4, 15, and 17). In perceiving things, in perceiving the world that comes to us, that is offered to us, that is *given to us*, we are certainly "passive"; that is, we receive something; but when we are affected, our responding activity is set in motion, thanks to which the object becomes experience, becomes "ours," becomes "us." It is certainly an action/reaction relationship, but within it opens the most amazing (though the least conspicuous, the most "normal") way to reach the consciousness of the receptor, and of the re-actor as an "I" every time. The ability to perceive the datum of reality coincides with the very possibility of arriving at oneself as provoked by being. Called into being down to one's own flesh (chapter 7). Beginning here, the impact, the contact, the given are charged with a possible meaning for me. Nature becomes history, experience, "consciousness."

(b) The second relevant point, which also cuts across the various passages attempted above (especially in chapters 3, 6, and 13), consists in our *faculty of desiring*: the lack that postpones, or rather constitutes, the irreducible trace of the presence of what we lack, as a lack that attracts and excites us. Desire is, as it were, the realization of self *as* lack, but of a lack that can never be rubricated among cases of "need" or "necessity," for the simple reason that any determined satisfaction that is procured for our urgencies can never come to grips with the inexhaustibility of desire. It can never nullify it. Desire is, by its very constitution, nothing less than a desire "to be," to be there. Before or even beyond any decision of the will or performance anxiety or pathology of dissatisfaction, desire attests that the experience of human beings is "made" *of* another, and shows a possible way to recognize that we are permanently made *of* another. In other words, desire is that maximally shared experience of humans that provides a "positive" meaning to a term otherwise definable only negatively, which is *infinity*. Desire by its very nature is infinite restlessness, unstoppable except at the price of denying any consistency to the self. Therefore, infinite desire does not only mean that it is continually recurring and always reborn after each partial or temporary satisfaction, but it can also mean that it is—consciously or unconsciously—a *desire for the infinite*. Only with the lexicon of desire, not with that of concepts or emotions alone, can the word "infinite" be sensibly and reasonably said from experience.

(c) A third point of irreducibility that emerged in the preceding chronicles is closely related to the issue just indicated of the infinite, and consists in the *acceptance of the self as a finite but free being*, that is, not *first and foremost* as an entity that will cease to exist with death, but first and foremost as an entity that came freely into the world, that "began" to be—that was *born*. Birth (discussed in chapter 8) is the irreversible attestation that our self is always lagging behind itself, because its origin is never simply at its disposal. The self in fact "is" its provenance, and paradoxically only as such can it be its own master. Being-born would seem to be the very negation of freedom, and instead it is its most vertiginous condition. Indeed, the albeit basic aspect of freedom as self-determination (or in-determination of the will) would still be too little to truly safeguard our being free. This is evidenced by the fact that those who believe that they are not conditioned by anything or anyone else in their decisions can always be argued against by way of the claim that, in fact, even our voluntary acts are determined from top to bottom by direct or indirect causes. *The experience of freedom* requires something else (I discuss this in chapters 5, 19, and 20): it requires the conscious act of agreeing to *be*, of consenting to the fact that we are there, even before we decide whether and how we can be what we would like to be. But it is possible to accept being not out of a resigned habituation to the given fact, but on the contrary because we sense that we are not enough for ourselves, that is, when we become aware of our coming not only in the initial sense, but as a permanent dimension of our being. "Coming" means not only not being the origin of ourselves, but having an ontological relationship with an origin that gives me to myself, wants me, loves me. This being "wanted" and "loved" is what is really at stake in the question of the meaning of self: it cannot be satisfied with a mythical or sentimental or uplifting solution, but expects to see "with open eyes" (chapter 16) the attestation, or more radically, the embodiment of that love that makes us be. Indeed, to be more precise, only if we recognize the constitutive link between love (being-wanted) and being in our personal existence can we meaningfully conceive it as the whole of reality. The counterevidence is that outside of that nexus, love is reduced to emotional feeling, and being to an unbearable, absurd case.

(d) All of this makes us regain another of the decisive points of our course, namely, that the problem of nihilism is primarily *a cognitive problem* rather than a problem of practical behavior or moral insufficiency.

Even in its historical origins, with the Russians and with Nietzsche, the problem has never been, "So what are we to do?" but, "So what is or is not really in the world?" And it is only by starting from the second problem that we can come to grips with the first. From this perspective we can better understand the canonical solutions that have been affirmed in the age of nihilism, and at the same time the gnoseological, epistemological, ethical, and sociopolitical problems that continually resurface beyond those supposed solutions. At the cognitive level, two pairs of opposing concepts are emblematic: that of knowledge and affection (chapter 5) and that of truth and certainty (chapter 10). They carry within them the modern inheritance that knowledge is objective measurement ("true") while affect is subjective feeling ("certain"), but at the same time raising the question of their intrinsic connection with a new challenge: to consider them independently would lead to misrecognizing both. Not only cognitive science but also cultural anthropology and a sociology of knowledge lead to a reevaluation of their constitutive nexus. The objectively measured world and the subjectively felt world are both abstractions; they are unreal in themselves. Only in their relationship to each other can they be realized as an actual experience of the world and self. As has repeatedly emerged in the course of our journey, reality cannot be reduced simply to what is there—outside or against the knowing subject. Nor can it be resolved by reducing the mind to a natural mechanism, or the world to a mental projection. Before any distinction and differentiation, and indeed precisely in order to be able to distinguish and differentiate the different planes, one must start from their constitutive ontological relation: it is because of it that one can consider them as poles in reaction. This relationship has taken on, in our reconnaissance, the scabrous and fascinating name of "mystery" (chapter 9). It is a mystery, that original relationship, not because it is nonexistent or unattainable or fideistically invented, but because it locates the invisible matrix of the visible, not simply that which is unseen and cannot be seen but that without which we could not see what we see. Again, we—finite as we are in our knowledge—always arrive too late to grasp the point of origin. But as we get to know things, we discover what binds us to them, that is, the mysterious relationship between the giving of the world and the opening of our selves.

(e) Finally, it is in morality itself, understood as the field of obligation, and in ethics as the territory of praxis and customs that nihilism
proves its victory as a shared conception, and at the same time its inadequacy with respect to the most radical demands of human existence. The
first of these demands, which in the nihilist type is perhaps even more
highlighted, is *the demand for happiness* (chapter 11). At first, the nihilists'
heated polemic against formal moral law and unconditional duty was carried out precisely in the name of claiming an amoral or antimoral (pure
will without form) happiness. But happiness is also an experience—even
if only in the form of a quest or a claim—that is always irreducible, like
freedom. It cannot simply be "decided," much less "produced" by us. A
programmed freedom or planned happiness would lead—as we have unfortunately seen historically—to the violence of a totalitarian ideology.
This is the paradox: all human life basically tends toward a supreme goal
of being happy, and yet nothing in the world can strategically produce
that goal, neither morality, nor culture, nor politics. They may help to
contain or curb the certain or probable causes of unhappiness, but it itself, happiness, remains unproducible and nondeducible from our will.
This suggests that there is always an irretrievable gap, an unbridgeable
gap between intention and realization, between expectation and fulfillment. Therefore, while the formalist morality of legality has sought to ex-
punge reference to the individual and personal interest from the search
for happiness, in order to achieve a general duty, on the other hand, being
happy has been transformed into a real "right" to be secured through state
legislation (discussed in chapter 14). Either outside the law or protected
by law, happiness remains another aporia of nihilism, literally a problem
with no possibility of solution—in the precise sense that only an "other"
than us can make us happy, and that therefore the path of morality is un-
derpinned by the tension of encountering and sharing this otherness.

These are just some of the problems that have emerged from time to
time in my chronicles. They already constitute a first answer to the question of what still remains to be thought about from the, so to speak, consummated experience of nihilism in our time. But in the face of them,
will it not also be necessary to indicate a *way of solution*, a possibility of
escape from the crisis of nihilism? What position to take in this situation
of epochal transition?

First, one must have the patience and intellectual courage to take seriously the *irreducible* character of these questions. It means that such demands of thought and action—the perception of the real and the consistency of the self, the desire to be, the experience of freedom, the mysterious unity of the mind and the world, the happiness of the individual as a relationship with the other—are permanent, and can never find a final satisfaction that would annul them as demands. After all, nihilism, in its various versions, has always had the temptation (as has emerged several times in the pages of this book) to overcome the crisis due to the lack of an ultimate sense of self and world by trying to grieve for that lack with a new creation of values and goals that would fill it. But it was always an illusory strategy: effective in many cases in establishing a new cultural and social order, but ultimately losing its goal, precisely because it "loses" those irreducible needs that constitute the experience of the human. The irreducible aspect of the self lies in the fact that nothing can fulfill it, that everything is "too little" for its realization. Recognizing this, however, does not at all mean remaining suspended indefinitely before one's own impossibility, but being available, so to speak, to the *impossible*. That is, open to the possibility that from outside of us someone or something will reach us as if from nowhere (see chapter 12), touching us and calling us precisely to be ourselves.

Now, the first form of this call of the real is our *ability to question*. But human questions are aroused by the encounter or impact with something that happens, by a shock or surprise of the real. "Why this?" or "How did this happen?" or "What are you asking me?" are the beginning of a journey that is not just a going in search of solutions for our issues but, if I may say so, a looking for the right questions to the answers that the real gives us. Rather than saying, "I have an answer for all your questions," a philosopher should rather say, "I have a question for all your answers." Only when the world allows itself to be questioned, and when we are willing to be questioned by it, do the self and the world "happen" in the proper sense.

The solution to the crisis of nihilism coincides with realizing the most obvious but also least recognized thing: realizing that we are there in the world. Not to emphasize our will to power, but to reclaim the original power of our self that coincides with our relationship with being. A power that paradoxically coincides with the capacity to receive the world, which is never a mere recording of data, but is the capacity to see—and also to hear, to touch—the presence of things that are given to us. In this presence of things the meaning we seek is offered. That is, meaning is not our own addition or construction, not a value or goal that we assign to things, but is the response to the presence of the real that calls us to participate in its giving. I would like in this regard to recall two exceptional witnesses who make one understand the whole impressiveness and at the same time the whole vibration of this experience of the presence of the world that is offered to us in its "sense." This is a comment that the poet Rainer Maria Rilke wrote, in a 1907 letter to his wife Clara from Paris, on the painting of Paul Cézanne. The German poet empathizes, with a giddy human sympathy—I would say, a metaphysical sympathy—with the creative tension of the French painter, who always aimed at the "realization" (*réalisation*) of his sensations, in particular to render the presence of things through his gaze at nature. Here the gaze is an intense *work of consciousness*: in the most immediate perception, the whole depth of the world is played out. It is not the vision that creates the world, which remains other than it; but at the same time the world in its very otherness is "realized" through our gaze. Indeed, it asks, it begs for our gaze in order to "be":

> . . . seeing and working—how different they are here. Everywhere else you see, and think: later—. Here they're almost one and the same. You're back again: that's not strange, not remarkable, not striking; it's not even a celebration; for a celebration would already be an interruption. But this here takes you and goes further with you and goes with you to everything and right through everything, through small things and great. Everything that was rearranges itself, lines up in formation, as if someone were standing there giving orders; and whatever is present is utterly and urgently present, as if prostrate on its knees and praying for you." (Hôtel du Quai Voltaire, Monday, June 3, 1907)

It is not we who ask nature to speak to us; it is the presence of things that asks us to look at them in order to communicate their truth to us.

Thus accepting the challenge posed by the nihilism of our time also means distancing oneself sharply from two other "ways out" of the crisis that seem most practiced: that of habituation and that of reaction. Both would fall short of the challenge because both would lose the urgency of the irreducible questions of experience. The first group, the addicts, accept nihilism as an irreversible destiny and as a planetary trend in Western culture, taking as definitive the assertion that one can be free only by somehow freeing oneself from the overly demanding burden of truth. Except then, one recognizes that from truth one cannot take leave with impunity by leaving the field open to blatant falsehood (I have discussed this in chapters 4, 10, and 13, including about fake news) and then proposing a reduction of truth to a procedure of political correctness. Once detached from each other, truth and freedom will always continue to look at each other with suspicion. Conversely, those who are merely reactive, or precisely "reactionary," overthrow the crisis by wanting to reaffirm truth without freedom. This is, if you will, the principle of all fundamentalism, which is inadequate not so much and not only because it disavows the weight of freedom, but precisely because it equivocates the nature of truth. If in order to recognize truth one had to impose it (on oneself and others), this would mean that truth does not have the inherent power to attest and win us over. For even the locution "The truth will make you free" not *only* means that our freedom must be based on truth values, but also and *especially* that truth is never attested to only by doctrinal or dialectical means, but to the extent that it makes us free. One can read that sentence like this: only if *I ground myself* in truth can I be free! But one can also read it in this other way: if something is true I realize it because it *sets me free*!

Paradoxically, if we can give nihilism any credit, it is that it has helped us to free the problem of truth from fundamentalism. But also to realize that rejecting the objectivity of truth is only an apparent alternative, because it would solve the problem of why things happen by simply denying it as a problem. Instead, the point to focus on is precisely that of the possibility of being free by acknowledging meaning. But it is precisely in this *free* realization of the true—of the irreducibility of the self and the astonishing presence of the real—that we can help nihilism understand its deepest need: that of overcoming itself.

BIBLIOGRAPHY

Chapter 1. Introduction to the American Edition:
For a Cartography of the Nihilism of Our Time

Dostoyevsky, Fyodor. *The Brothers Karamazov*. 1879. Translated by Constance Garnett. Revised by Ralph E. Matlaw. New York: Norton, 2011.

———. *The Demons*. 1873. Translated by Robert A. Maguire. Edited by Ronald Meyer. London: Penguin Classics, 2008.

Dreyfus, Hubert L. *Being-in-the-World: A Commentary on Heidegger's "Being and Time," Division I*. Cambridge, MA: MIT Press, 1991.

Dreyfus, Hubert L., and Sean Dorrance Kelly. *All Things Shining: Reading the Western Classics to Find Meaning in a Secular Age*. New York: Free Press, 2011.

Esposito, Costantino. "The Link between 'Fundamentalism' and 'Relativism.'" In *Retrieving Origins and the Claim of Multiculturalism*, translated by Mariangela Sullivan, 44–56. Grand Rapids, MI: Eerdmans, 2014.

Gertz, Nolen. *Nihilism*. Cambridge, MA: MIT Press, 2019.

Gillespie, Michael Allen. *Nihilism before Nietzsche*. Chicago: University of Chicago Press, 1995.

Habermas, Jürgen. "Hans-Georg Gadamer: Urbanizing the Heideggerian Province." In *Philosophical-Political Profiles*, translated by Frederick G. Lawrence, 191–99. Cambridge, MA: MIT Press, 1989.

Habermas, Jürgen, and Joseph Ratzinger. *The Dialectics of Secularization: On Reason and Religion*. Translated by Brian McNeil. San Francisco: Ignatius, 2007.

Jacobi, Friedrich Heinrich. "Open Letter to Fichte, 1799." Translated by D. I. Behler. In *Philosophy of German Idealism*, edited by Ernst Behler, 119–41. New York: Continuum, 1987.

Lyotard, Jean-François. *The Postmodern Condition: A Report on Knowledge*. Translated by Geoffrey Bennington and Brian Massumi. Manchester, UK: Manchester University Press, 1984.

MacCormack, Patricia. *The Ahuman Manifesto: Activism for the End of the Anthropocene*. London: Bloomsbury Academic, 2020.

Milbank, John. *The Future of Love: Essays in Political Theology.* London: SCM, 2009.

Nietzsche, Friedrich. *Twilight of the Idols, or How to Philosophize with a Hammer.* 1889. Translated by Duncan Large. Oxford: Oxford University Press, 2008.

Panaïoti, Antoine. *Nietzsche and Buddhist Philosophy.* Cambridge: Cambridge University Press, 2013.

Rorty, Richard. *Consequences of Pragmatism (Essays: 1972–1980).* Minneapolis: University of Minnesota Press, 1982.

———. *Philosophy and the Mirror of Nature.* Princeton: Princeton University Press, 1979.

———. "Response to John McDowell: Towards Rehabilitating Objectivity." In *Rorty and His Critics,* edited by Robert B. Brandom, 123–28. Oxford: Blackwell, 2000.

———. Review of *Nihilism,* by Stanley Rosen. *Philosophy Forum* 11 (1972): 102–8.

Rosen, Stanley. *Nihilism: A Philosophical Essay.* New Haven: Yale University Press, 1969.

Rowe, Aidan. "Gender Nihilism." In *What Is Gender Nihilism? A Reader,* 341–47. Seattle: Contagion Press, 2019.

Schleiermacher, Friedrich Daniel Ernst. *On Religion: Speeches to Its Cultured Despisers.* 1799. Edited by Richard Crouter. Cambridge: Cambridge University Press, 1996.

Schürmann, Reiner. *Heidegger on Being and Acting: From Principles to Anarchy.* Translated by Christine-Marie Gros. Bloomington: Indiana University Press, 1987.

Searle, John. *Intentionality: An Essay in the Philosophy of Mind.* Cambridge: Cambridge University Press, 1983.

Taylor, Charles. *A Secular Age.* Cambridge, MA: Belknap Press, 2007.

Turgenev, Ivan. *Fathers and Sons.* Translated by Constance Garnett. Oxford: Oxford University Press, 2008.

Vattimo, Gianni. *Beyond Interpretation: The Meaning of Hermeneutics for Philosophy.* Translated by David Webb. Cambridge: Polity Press, 1997.

———. *Il soggetto e la maschera: Nietzsche e il problema della liberazione* [The subject and the mask: Nietzsche and the problem of liberation]. Milan: Bompiani, 1974.

———. *Nihilism and Emancipation: Ethics, Politics and Law.* Edited by Santiago Zabala. New York: Columbia University Press, 2007.

———. *Of Reality: The Purposes of Philosophy.* Translated by Robert T. Valgenti. New York: Columbia University Press, 2016.

———. *The Transparent Society.* Translated by David Webb. Baltimore: Johns Hopkins University Press, 1992.

Warren, Calvin L. *Ontological Terror: Blackness, Nihilism, and Emancipation.* Durham, NC: Duke University Press, 2018.

Weber, Max. *Science as a Vocation*. 1917. Edited by Peter Lassman and Irving Velody. Milton Park, UK: Taylor & Francis, 2015.

Zuckerman, Phil. *Living the Secular Life: New Answers to Old Questions*. London: Penguin Press, 2014.

Chapter 2. Nihilism, Zero Point

McCarthy, Cormac. *The Road*. New York: Knopf, 2006.

Chapter 3. Glimmers in the Dark

Del Noce, Augusto. *The Crisis of Modernity*. Edited and translated by Carlo Lancellotti. Montreal: McGill-Queen's University Press, 2014.

———. *Il suicidio della rivoluzione* [The suicide of revolution]. 1978. Edited by Giuseppe Riconda. Turin: Nino Aragno Editore, 2004.

Dostoyevsky, Fyodor. *The Brothers Karamazov*. 1879. Translated by Constance Garnett. Revised by Ralph E. Matlaw. New York: Norton, 2011.

Eco, Umberto. *Foucault's Pendulum*. 1988. Boston: Mariner Books, 2007.

Esposito, Costantino. "Heidegger e il nichilismo europeo" [Heidegger and European nihilism]. *Acta Philosophica* 26 (2017): 105–22.

Houellebecq, Michel. *Serotonin*. Translated by Shaun Whiteside. New York: Picador, 2020.

Nietzsche, Friedrich. *The Will to Power*. Translated by Walter Kaufmann and R. J. Hollingdale. New York: Vintage Books, 1968.

Vercellone, Federico. *Introduzione al nichilismo* [Introduction to nihilism]. Rome: Laterza, 2009.

Verra, Valerio. "Nichilismo" [Nihilism]. In *Enciclopedia del Novecento*, 4:778–90. 4 vols. Rome: Istituto dell'Enciclopedia Italiana, 1979.

Volpi, Franco. *Il nichilismo* [Nihilism]. Rome: Laterza, 2018.

Chapter 4. Intelligence Is Not Autopilot

Cassese, Sabino. 2018. "La cattiva politica schiava della percezione" [The bad policy enslaved by perception]. *7* [weekly magazine of the newspaper *Corriere della sera*], September 13, 2018.

Disegni, Simone. 2018. "Cibo, salute, criminalità, disoccupati: È l'Italia il Paese che sa meno di sé" [Food, health, crime, unemployment: Italy is the country that knows least about itself]. *Corriere della sera*, August 31, 2018.

Doctorow, Cory. "Three Kinds of Propaganda, and What to Do about Them." *Boing Boing*, February 25th, 2017, https://boingboing.net/2017/02/25 /counternarratives-not-fact-che.html.

Dreyfus, Hubert L. *What Computers Can't Do: The Limits of Artificial Intelligence*. New York: HarperCollins, 1978.

Heidegger, Martin. "Science and Reflection." 1953. In *The Question concerning Technology, and Other Essays*, edited by William Lovitt, 155–82. New York: Garland, 1977.

Recalcati, Massimo. *Ritratti del desiderio* [Portraits of desire]. Milan: Raffaello Cortina, 2018.

Steinmetz, Katy. "How Your Brain Tricks You into Believing Fake News." *Time*, August 9, 2018. https://time.com/5362183/the-real-fake-news-crisis/.

Weil, Simone. *Waiting for God*. New York: Harper Perennial, 1973.

Chapter 5. That Gap between Knowledge and Affection

Alighieri, Dante. *The Divine Comedy of Dante Alighieri*. Edited and translated by Robert M. Durling. Oxford: Oxford University Press, 2011.

Nietzsche, Friedrich. *The Will to Power*. Translated by Walter Kaufmann and R. J. Hollingdale. New York: Vintage Books, 1968.

Remotti, Francesco. *Contro natura: Una lettera al Papa* [Against nature: A letter to the pope]. Rome: Laterza 2008.

Wallace, David Foster. *This Is Water: Some Thoughts, Delivered on a Significant Occasion, about Living a Compassionate Life*. New York: Little, Brown, 2009.

Zambrano, María. *Hacia un saber sobre el alma* [Toward a knowledge of the soul]. 1950. Madrid: Alianza Editorial, 2019.

Chapter 6. The Infinity Within

Deleuze, Gilles. *Pure Immanence: Essays on a Life*. Translated by A. Boyman. New York: Zone Books, 2001. Originally published in 1995 as *L'immanence: Une vie*.

Descartes, René. *Meditations on First Philosophy, with Selections from the Objections and Replies*. 1641. Translated by M. Moriarty. Oxford: Oxford University Press, 2008.

Francis (Pope). *Laudato Si': On Care for Our Common Home*. Encyclical letter. Vatican City: Vatican Press, 2015.

Leopardi, Giacomo. "Canto notturno di un pastore errante dell'Asia" [Night song of a wandering shepherd in Asia]. 1831. In *Canti*, translated and annotated by Johnathan Galassi. London: Penguin Books, 2010.

Lévinas, Emmanuel. *Totality and Infinity: An Essay on Exteriority*. Translated by A. Lingis. Pittsburgh: Duquesne University Press, 1961.

Nietzsche, Friedrich. *The Gay Science: With a Prelude in German Rhymes and an Appendix of Songs*. 1887. Translated by Josefine Nauckhoff and Adrian del Caro. Edited by Bernard Williams. Cambridge: Cambridge University Press, 2008.

Pasqualotto, Giangiorgio. *Dieci lezioni sul buddhismo* [Ten lectures on Buddhism]. Venice: Marsilio, 2017.

Spinoza, Baruch. *Ethics*. 1677. In *Complete Works*, translated by Samuel Shirley, edited, with introduction and notes, by Michael L. Morgan, 213–382. Indianapolis: Hackett, 2002.

Chapter 7. The Vocation of the Flesh

Agamben, Giorgio. *The Omnibus Homo Sacer*. Stanford, CA: Stanford University Press, 2017.

Carrón, Julian. *The Radiance in Your Eyes: What Saves Us from Nothingness?* Translated by Sheila Beatty. Tampa: Human Adventure Books, 2020.

Chiappini, Rudy, ed. *Bacon*. Milan: Skira, 2008.

Faietti, Marzia, and Matteo Lafranconi, eds. *Raphael, 1520–1483*. Milan: Skira, 2020.

Foucault, Michel. *The Birth of Biopolitics: Lectures at the College de France, 1978–1979*. New York: Palgrave Macmillan, 2011.

Freud, Sigmund. *The Standard Edition of the Complete Psychological Works*. 24 vols. Edited by James Strachey, in collaboration with Anna Freud, assisted by Alix Strachey and Alan Tyson. New York: Norton, 1976.

Groddeck, Georg. *The Book of the It*. 1923. New York: Vintage Books, 1949.

Henry, Michel. *Incarnation: A Philosophy of Flesh*. 2000. Translated by Karl Hefty. Evanston, IL: Northwestern University Press, 2015.

Husserl, Edmund. *Cartesian Meditations: An Introduction to Phenomenology*. 1931. Translated by Dorian Cairns. Berlin: Springer, 2013.

Maubert, Franck. *L'odeur du sang humain ne me quitte pas des yeux: Conversations avec Francis Bacon* [The smell of human blood never leaves my eyes: Conversations with Francis Bacon]. Paris: Mille et une nuits, 2009.

Merleau-Ponty, Maurice. *Phenomenology of Perception*. 1945. Translated by Donald A. Landes. London: Routledge, 2012.

Nietzsche, Friedrich. *Thus Spoke Zarathustra*. 1885. Edited by Adrian del Caro and Robert B. Pippin. Cambridge: Cambridge University Press, 2006.

Schmitt, Carl. *Political Theology: Four Chapters on the Concept of Sovereignty*. 1922. Translated by George Schwab. Chicago: University of Chicago Press, 2005.

Schopenhauer, Arthur. *The World as Will and Representation*. 1859. Vol. 1. Translated and edited by Judith Norman, Alistair Welchman, and Christopher Janaway with an introduction by Christopher Janaway. Cambridge: Cambridge University Press, 2010.

Chapter 8. *The Gratitude of Being Born*

Arendt, Hannah. *Between Past and Future: Six Exercises in Political Thought*. New York: Viking Press, 1961.

Arendt, Hannah, and Karl Jaspers. *Correspondence, 1926–1969*. Edited by Lotte Kohler and Hans Saner. San Diego: Harcourt, 1985.

Finkielkraut, Alain. *L'ingratitude: Conversation sur notre temps* [Ingratitude: A conversation about our times]. Paris: Gallimard, 1999.

Heidegger, Martin. *Being and Time*. 1927. Translated by John Macquarrie and Edward Robinson. Oxford: Blackwell, 2001.

Stone, Alison. *Being Born: Birth and Philosophy*. Oxford: Oxford University Press, 2019.

Chapter 9. *Shock in the Face of Mystery*

Corà, Bruno, ed. *Burri: La pittura irriducibile presenza* [Painting as an irreducible presence]. Florence: Forma Edizioni, 2019.

Dennett, Daniel. *Sweet Dreams: Philosophical Obstacles to a Science of Consciousness*. Cambridge, MA: MIT Press, 2005.

Fontana, Lucio. *Manifesti Scritti Interviste* [Manifestos writings interviews]. Edited by Angela Sanna. Milan: Abscondita, 2015.

Formica, Giambattista. "Naturalismo, riduzionismo, eliminativismo: Considerazioni metodologiche sul problema del soggetto" [Naturalism, reductionism, eliminativism: Methodological considerations on the problem of the subject]. In *Filosofia dell'avvenire*, edited by Ugo Perone, 84–94. Turin: Rosenberg & Sellier, 2010.

Lacan, Jacques. *Reading Seminar XI: Lacan's Four Fundamental Concepts of Psychoanalysis*. 1964. Edited by Richard Feldstein, Bruce Fink, and Maire Jaanus. Albany: State University of New York Press, 1995.

Marcel, Gabriel. "On the Ontological Mystery." In *The Philosophy of Existentialism*, translated by Manya Harari, 9–46. New York: Citadel Press, 1970.

Searle, John. *Mind, Language and Society: Philosophy in the Real World*. New York: Basic Books, 1999.

———. *The Mystery of Consciousness*. New York: New York Review Books, 1997.

———. "Reply to 'Searle's Biological Naturalism: A Typology.'" In *John R. Searle: Thinking about the Real World*, edited by Dirk Franken, Attila Karakus, and Jan G. Michel, 210–14. Berlin: de Gruyter, 2010.

Wittgenstein, Ludwig. *Tractatus Logico-Philosophicus*. 1921. Edited by David F. Pears and Brian F. McGuinness. London: Routledge, 2001.

Chapter 10. The Distance between Certainty and Truth

Bauman, Zygmunt. *Liquid Fear*. Cambridge: Polity Press, 2006.

Beck, Ulrich. *World at Risk*. Translated by Ciaran Cronin. Cambridge: Polity Press, 2009.

Esposito, Costantino. "E l'esistenza diventa una immensa certezza" [And existence becomes an immense certainty]. In *Una certezza per l'esistenza*, edited by Emanuela Belloni and Alberto Savorana, 42–66. Milan: Rizzoli, 2011.

Ferraris, Maurizio. *Manifesto of New Realism*. Translated by Sarah De Sanctis. Albany: State University of New York Press, 2014.

Newman, John Henry. *An Essay in Aid of a Grammar of Assent*. London: Burns, Oates, & Co., 1874.

Vattimo, Gianni. *Of Reality: The Purposes of Philosophy*. Translated by Robert T. Valgenti. New York: Columbia University Press, 2016.

Wittgenstein, Ludwig. *On Certainty*. Edited by Gertrude Elizabeth Margaret Anscombe and Georg Henrik von Wright. New York: Harper Perennial, 1972.

Chapter 11. Ask Me If I'm Happy

Aristotle. *The Nicomachean Ethics*. Translated by David Ross. Oxford: Oxford University Press, 2009.

Augustine. *Confessions*. Translated by Henry Chadwick. Oxford: Oxford University Press, 1998.

Beeman, Richard, ed. *The Penguin Guide to the United States Constitution: A Fully Annotated Declaration of Independence, U.S. Constitution and Amendments, and Selections from "The Federalist Papers."* London: Penguin Books, 2010.

Epicurus. *The Epicurus Reader*. Translated and edited by Brad Inwood and Lloyd P. Gerson. Indianapolis: Hackett, 1994.

Esposito, Costantino, Giovanni Maddalena, Paolo Ponzio, and Massimiliano Savini, eds. *Felicità e desiderio: Letture di filosofia* [Happiness and desire: Philosophy readings]. Bari: Edizioni di Pagina, 2006.

Hadot, Pierre. *Philosophy as a Way of Life: Spiritual Exercises from Socrates to Foucault*. 1981. Edited by Arnold I. Davidson. Hoboken, NJ: Wiley-Blackwell, 1995.

Kant, Immanuel. *Critique of Practical Reason*. 1788. Translated by Werner S. Pluhar. Indianapolis: Hackett, 2002.

Marion, Jean-Luc. *Negative Certainties*. Translated by Stephen E. Lewis. Chicago: University of Chicago Press, 2015.

Natoli, Salvatore. *La salvezza senza fede* [Salvation without faith]. Milan: Feltrinelli, 2007.

Nietzsche, Friedrich. *Thus Spoke Zarathustra*. 1885. Edited by Adrian del Caro and Robert B. Pippin. Cambridge: Cambridge University Press, 2006.

Phillips, Todd, and Scott Silver. "Joker: An Origin." Movie script. 2018. Internet Movie Script Database. www.imsdb.com/scripts/Joker.html.

Reale, Giovanni. *La filosofia di Seneca come terapia dei mali dell'anima* [Seneca's philosophy as therapy for the pains of the soul]. Milan: Bompiani, 2003.

Richter, Gisela M. A. *Kouroi: Archaic Greek Youths; A Study of the Development of the Kouros Type in Greek Sculpture*. London: Phaidon, 1970.

Rilke, Rainer Maria. *"Duino Elegies" and "The Sonnets to Orpheus."* Translated by Alfred A. Poulin Jr. Boston: Houghton Mifflin, 1977.

Spinoza, Baruch. *Ethics*. 1677. In *Complete Works*, translated by Samuel Shirley, edited, with introduction and notes, by Michael L. Morgan, 213–382. Indianapolis: Hackett, 2002.

Chapter 12. That Drawing Hidden inside the Fog

Aristotle. *Metaphysics*. Edited and translated by C. D. C. Reeve. Indianapolis: Hackett, 2016.

Givone, Sergio. *Storia del nulla* [History of nothingness]. Rome: Laterza, 1995.

Eco, Umberto. "La filosofia di Eco: 'Il pensiero è un manuale senza confini'" [Eco's philosophy: 'Thought is a manual without boundaries']." Interview with Umberto Eco. By Antonio Gnoli. *la Repubblica*, February 20, 2014.

Heidegger, Martin. *What Is Metaphysics?* 1929. In *Pathmarks*, edited by William McNeill, 82–96. Cambridge: Cambridge University Press, 1998 [1967].

———. *Letter on "Humanism."* 1946. In *Pathmarks*, edited by William Mc-Neill, 239–76. Cambridge: Cambridge University Press, 1998 [1967].

Leibniz, Gottfried. *Monadology: A New Translation and Guide.* 1714. Edinburgh: Edinburgh University Press, 2014.

Liuzzi, Tiziana. *Viaggio in Inghilterra: L'Occidente al crocevia del nichilismo; Virginia Woolf, Chesterton, Tolkien* [Journey to England: The West at the crossroads of nihilism: Virginia Woolf, Chesterton, Tolkien. Bari: Edizioni di Pagina, 2010.

Montale, Eugenio. *Forse un mattino andando in un'aria di vetro* [Maybe one morning, walking in dry, glassy air]. 1923. In *Collected Poems, 1920–1954*, translated by Jonathan Galassi, 54–55. New York: Farrar, Straus and Giroux, 1988.

Novak, Michael. *The Experience of Nothingness.* New York: Harper & Row, 1971.

Pareyson, Luigi. *Ontologia della libertà: Il male e la sofferenza* [Ontology of freedom: The evil and the suffering]. Turin: Einaudi, 2000.

Parmenides. *The Fragments of Parmenides: A Critical Text with Introduction and Translation, the Ancient Testimonia and a Commentary.* Edited by Allan H. Coxon. Las Vegas: Parmenides Publishing, 2009.

Plato. *Sophist.* In *Complete Works*, edited by John M. Cooper, with associate editor D. S. Hutchinson, 235–93. Indianapolis: Hackett, 1997.

Sartre, Jean-Paul. *Being and Nothingness: An Essay in Phenomenological Ontology.* 1945. New York: Citadel Press, 2001.

Severino, Emanuele. *The Essence of Nihilism.* 1972. Translated by Giacomo Donis. Edited by Ines Testoni and Alessandro Carrera. London: Verso, 2016.

Woolf, Virginia. *Moments of Being.* 1939. San Diego: Harvest/HBJ, 1985.

Yao, Zhihua. *Nonexistent Objects in Buddhist Philosophy: On Knowing What There Is Not.* London: Bloomsbury Academic, 2020.

Chapter 13. On the Desire for Truth

Aquinas, St. Thomas. *Truth.* Translated by Robert W. Mulligan, James V. McGlynn, and Robert W. Schmidt. 3 vols. Chicago: H. Regnery Co., 1952–54. Original title: *Quaestiones disputatae de veritate.*

Balthasar, Hans Urs von. *Theo-Logic I: Truth of the World.* 1985. Translated by Adrian J. Walker. San Francisco: Ignatius, 2000.

Descartes, René. *A Discourse on the Method of Correctly Conducting One's Reason and Seeking Truth in the Sciences.* 1637. Translated by Ian Maclean. Oxford: Oxford University Press, 2006.

Esposito, Costantino. *Una ragione inquieta: Interventi e riflessioni nelle pieghe del nostro tempo* [A restless reason: Interventions and reflections in the folds of our time]. Bari: Edizioni di Pagina, 2011.

Latour, Bruno. *Rejoicing, or The Torments of Religious Speech*. Cambridge: Polity Press, 2013.

Nietzsche, Friedrich. *Ecce Homo: How to Become What You Are*. 1888. Translated by Duncan Large. Oxford: Oxford University Press, 2007.

———. *The Gay Science: With a Prelude in German Rhymes and an Appendix of Songs*. 1887. Translated by Josefine Nauckhoff and Adrian del Caro. Edited by Bernard Williams. Cambridge: Cambridge University Press, 2008.

Chapter 14. The Duty that Attracts

Kant, Immanuel. *Critique of Practical Reason*. 1788. Translated by Werner S. Pluhar. Indianapolis: Hackett, 2002.

Lessing, Gotthold Ephraim. *The Education of the Human Race*. 1780. In *Philosophical and Theological Writings*, translated and edited by Hugh Barr Nisbet, 217–40. Cambridge: Cambridge University Press, 2005.

Nietzsche, Friedrich. *Thus Spoke Zarathustra*. 1885. Edited by Adrian del Caro and Robert B. Pippin. Cambridge: Cambridge University Press, 2006.

Péguy, Charles. *Victor-Marie, Comte Hugo, Solvuntur objecta*. 1910. In *Œuvres en prose completes*, edited by Robert Burac, vol. 3 [1909–1914], 161–345. Paris: Gallimard, 1992.

Taylor, Charles. *The Malaise of Modernity*. Toronto: House of Anansi Press, 1991.

Violante, Luciano. *Il dovere di avere doveri* [The duty of having duties]. Turin: Einaudi, 2014.

———. "Ripartire dal fare comunità" [Restarting by making community]. *L'Osservatore Romano*, July 2, 2019.

Weber, Max. *The Vocation Lectures*. 1917–18. Translated by Rodney Livingstone. Edited by David Owen and Tracy B. Strong. Indianapolis: Hackett, 2004.

Chapter 15. That Emotion that Dwells in Reason: Inside Out

Baggini, Julian. "Inside Out: A Crash Course in PhD Philosophy of Self That Kids Will Get First." *Guardian*, July 27, 2015.

Damasio, Antonio. *Descartes' Error: Emotion, Reason, and the Human Brain*. London: Penguin Books, 2005.

Dawkins, Richard. *The Selfish Gene*. 1976. Oxford: Oxford University Press, 2006.

Descartes, René. *The Passions of the Soul, and Other Late Philosophical Writings*. 1649. Translated by Michael Moriarty. Oxford: Oxford University Press, 2015.

Docter, Pete, and Del Carmen Ronnie. "Inside Out." Movie script. 2015. Screenplay by Pete Docter, Meg LeFauve, and Josh Cooley. The Daily Script. https://www.dailyscript.com/scripts/inside-out-screenplay.pdf.

Esposito, Costantino. "Se l'io va fuori di sé" [If the ego is beside itself]. *Tracce*, November 2015, 39–41.

Hume, David. *A Treatise on Human Nature*. 1739–40. Vol. 1, *Texts*. Edited by David Fate Norton and Mary J. Norton. Oxford: Oxford University Press, 2007.

Kant, Immanuel. *Critique of the Power of Judgment*. 1790. Translated by Paul Guyer and Eric Matthews. Edited by Paul Guyer. Cambridge: Cambridge University Press.

Polito, Antonio. "Il film per ragazzi senza la ragione" [The children's movie without the reason]. *Corriere della sera*, October 4, 2015.

Plutchik, Robert. *The Psychology and Biology of Emotions*. 1968. New York: Harper Collins College, 1996.

Chapter 16. With What Eyes We Look at the World

Adorno, Theodor W. *Aesthetic Theory*. Translated by Robert Hullot-Kentor. London: Continuum, 2002.

Augustine. *Confessions*. Translated by Henry Chadwick. Oxford: Oxford University Press, 1998.

Calvino, Italo. *The Baron in the Trees*. 1957. Translated by Ann Goldstein. Boston: Mariner Books, 2017.

———. *Letters, 1941–1985*. Translated by Martin McLaughlin. Edited by Michael Wood. Princeton: Princeton University Press, 2014.

———. *Mr Palomar*. Translated by William Weaver. London: Secker & Warburg, 1985.

———. *Six Memos for the Next Millennium*. New York: Vintage International Books, 1993.

———. *T Zero*. Translated by William Weaver. San Diego: Harcourt Brace Jovanovich, 1976.

———. *The Uses of Literature*. Translated by Patrick Creagh. Boston: Mariner Books, 1987.

Esposito, Costantino, Giovanni Maddalena, Paolo Ponzio, and Massimiliano Savini, eds. *Beauty and Reality: Philosophy Readings*. Bari: Edizioni di Pagina, 2007.

Chapter 17. The Loss of the Ego, the Reconquest of the Self

Augustine. *Confessions.* Translated by Henry Chadwick. Oxford: Oxford University Press, 1998.

Crick, Francis. *The Astonishing Hypothesis: The Scientific Search for the Soul.* London: Simon & Schuster, 1994.

Dennett, Daniel C. *Consciousness Explained.* New York: Back Bay Books, 1991.

Houellebecq, Michel. *Extension du domaine de la lutte.* Paris: Éditions Maurice Nadeau, 1994.

Hume, David. *A Treatise on Human Nature.* 1739–40. Vol. 1, *Texts.* Edited by David Fate Norton and Mary J. Norton. Oxford: Oxford University Press, 2007.

Koch, Christof. *The Quest for Consciousness: A Neurobiological Approach.* Englewood, Co: Roberts & Co., 2004.

Nietzsche, Friedrich. *The Will to Power.* Translated by Walter Kaufmann and R. J. Hollingdale. New York: Vintage Books, 1968.

Pirandello, Luigi. *Six Characters in Search of an Author.* 1921. In *Three Plays*, translated by Anthony Mortimer. Oxford: Oxford University Press, 2014.

Ricoeur, Paul. *Oneself as Another.* Translated by Kathleen Blamey. Chicago: University of Chicago Press, 1992.

Roth, Philip. *The Counterlife.* New York: Vintage Books, 1996.

Sacks, Oliver. *The River of Consciousness.* New York: Knopf, 2017.

Chapter 18. An Ambiguous Power: The Technical Face of Nihilism

Baricco, Alessandro. *The Game: A Digital Turning Point.* Translated by Clarissa Botsford. San Francisco: McSweeney, 2020.

Borgna, Eugenio. *La nostalgia ferita* [The wounded nostalgia]. Turin: Einaudi, 2018.

Clark, Andy. *Natural-Born Cyborgs: Minds, Technologies, and the Future of Human Intelligence.* Oxford: Oxford University Press, 2004.

Descartes, René. *Meditations on First Philosophy, with Selections from the Objections and Replies.* 1641. Translated by M. Moriarty. Oxford: Oxford University Press, 2008.

Di Francesco, Michele, and Giulia Piredda. *La mente estesa: Dove finisce la mente e comincia il resto del mondo?* [The extended mind: Where does the mind end and the rest of the world begin?]. Milan: Mondadori Università, 2012.

Ferrari, Marco, ed. *Logos e techne* [*Logos* and *techne*]. Milan: Mimesis, 2017.

Ferraris, Maurizio. *Mobilitazione totale* [Total mobilization]. Rome: Laterza, 2015.

Floridi, Luciano. *Il verde e il blu: Idee ingenue per migliorare la politica* [The green and the blue: Naive ideas to improve politics]. Milan: Raffaello Cortina, 2020.

Galimberti, Umberto. *Psiche e techne: L'uomo nell'età della tecnica* [Psyche and techne: Man in the age of technique]. Milan: Feltrinelli, 1999.

Gehlen, Arnold. *Man: His Nature and Place in the World*. 1940. Translated by Clare McMillan and Karl Pillemer. New York: Columbia University Press, 1988.

Heidegger, Martin. "The Question concerning Technology." 1953. In *The Question concerning Technology, and Other Essays*. Edited by William Lovitt. New York: Garland, 1977.

Heidegger, Martin, and Ernst Jünger. *Correspondence, 1949–1975*. London: Rowman & Littlefield, 2016.

Hölderlin, Friedrich. "Patmos." 1807. In *Poems* selected and translated by James Mitchell, 39–45. San Francisco: Ithuriel's Spear, 2004.

Jünger, Ernst. "Total Mobilization." In *The Heidegger Controversy: A Critical Reader*, edited by Wolin, Richard, 119–39. Cambridge, MA: MIT Press, 1993.

Latouche, Serge. *Le pari de la décroissance* [The challenge of degrowth]. Paris: Fayard, 2006.

Leopardi, Giacomo. "Canto notturno di un pastore errante dell'Asia" [Night song of a wandering shepherd in Asia]. 1831. In *Canti*, translated and annotated by Johnathan Galassi. London: Penguin Books, 2010.

Mazzarella, Eugenio. *L'uomo che deve rimanere: La 'smoralizzazione' del mondo* [The man who must remain: The 'demoralisation' of the world]. Macerata: Quodlibet, 2017.

Morin, Edgar. *Penser global: L'homme et son univers* [Global thought: Man and his universe]. Paris: Éditions Robert Laffont, 2015.

Nietzsche, Friedrich. *The Will to Power*. Translated by Walter Kaufmann and R. J. Hollingdale. New York: Vintage Books, 1968.

Severino, Emanuele. *Il destino della tecnica* [The destiny of the technique]. 1998. Milan: Rizzoli, 2011.

Sini, Carlo. *L'uomo, la macchina, l'automa: Lavoro e conoscenza tra futuro prossimo e passato remoto* [The man, the machine, the robot: Work and knowledge between the near future and the distant past]. Turin: Bollati Boringhieri, 2009.

Zuboff, Shoshana. *The Age of Surveillance Capitalism: The Fight for a Human Future at the New Frontier of Power*. New York: PublicAffairs, 2019.

Chapter 19. Rust, Dolores, and the Enigma of Freedom

Berlin, Isaiah. *Freedom and Its Betrayal: Six Enemies of Human Liberty*. Edited by Henry Hardy. Princeton: Princeton University Press, 2014.

De Caro, Mario. *Il libero arbitrio: Una introduzione* [Free will: An introduction]. 2004. Rome: Laterza, 2019.

De Caro, Mario, Massimo Mori, and Emidio Spinelli, eds. *Libero arbitrio: Storia di una controversia filosofica* [Free will: History of a philosopical controversy]. Rome: Carocci, 2014.

Esposito, Costantino, Giovanni Maddalena, Paolo Ponzio, and Massimiliano Savini, eds. *Il potere della libertà: Letture di filosofia* [The power of freedom: Philosophy readings]. Bari: Edizioni di Pagina, 2008.

Graham, Jacob, and Tom Sparrow, eds. *True Detective and Philosophy: A Deeper Kind of Darkness*. Hoboken, NJ: Wiley-Blackwell, 2018.

Kant, Immanuel. *Groundwork of the Metaphysick of Moral*. 1785. Translated and edited by Mary Gregor. Cambridge: Cambridge University Press, 1997.

Illuminati, Augusto, ed. *Averroè e l'intelletto pubblico: Antologia di scritti di Ibn Rushd sull'anima* [Averroes and the public intellect: Anthology of Ibn Rushd's writings on the soul]. Rome: Manifestolibri, 1996.

List, Christian. *Why Free Will Is Real*. Cambridge, MA: Harvard University Press, 2019.

Lucci, Antonio. *True Detective: Una filosofia al negativo* [True detective: A negative philosophy]. Genoa: il melangolo, 2019.

Montale, Eugenio. *In limine* [On the threshold]. 1925. In *Collected Poems, 1920–1954*, translated by Jonathan Galassi, 4–5. New York: Farrar, Straus and Giroux, 1988.

Reale, Giovanni, and Elisabetta Sgarbi. *I misteri di Grünewald e dell'altare di Isenheim: Una interpretazione storico-ermeneutica* [The mysteries of Grünewald and the Isenheim Altar: A historical-hermeneutic interpretation]. Milan: Bompiani, 2008.

Chapter 20. Rue in Free Fall

Augustine. *On Free Choice of the Will*. Translated by Thomas Williams. Indianapolis: Hackett, 1993.

Chapter 21. Conclusion: What Answers Do We Need?

Rilke, Rainer Maria. *Letters on Cézanne*. Edited by Clara Rilke. Translated by Joel Agee. Berkeley, CA: North Point Press, 2002.

INDEX OF NAMES

INDEX OF TERMS

reductionism, x, 23, 36, 38, 64–65,
    105, 116, 119–20, 122, 127,
    143–44, 168
relativism, 4, 8, 16, 74, 91, 94, 95
religion, 2, 16–17, 25, 92–93
    critique of, 11–14, 44, 48
rights, 4, 13, 33, 71, 96–97, 165
    age of, 95
    civil, 21
    and duty (*see under* duty)
    to happiness, 74
    society of (*see under* society)
Romanticism, 5, 37, 137

S
sacred, 15–17, 46
secularization, 4–6, 10–17, 105, 123,
    132
    secular society, 12–13
seeing, 107–8, 113
Self, 2, 7, 12, 16, 26–27, 41,
    48–49
    alienation and recovery of, 119
    biological, 116, 119–20
    bundle theory of (*see under*
        consciousness)
    construction of (*see under*
        construction)
    critique of the ego as subject,
        115
    deconstruction of, 115, 117
    determination of, 6, 13, 95, 105,
        144, 163
    fluid identity of, 106, 115
    irreducibility of, 34, 37–38, 49–50,
        59, 106, 115, 161, 168
    loss of, 35, 118
    narcissistic, 72

narrative, 69, 76, 102–3, 116, 119
    nihilistic, 114–17, 119
    nostalgia of, 137
    performative identity of, 139
    performative linguistic act of "I"
        (*see under* language)
    realization of, 14, 25
    solipsistic, 50
    suppression of, 6, 34, 115
sex, 22, 34, 54, 88, 95, 151, 156
society, 4, 23, 38, 48, 57, 62
    consumer, 33, 55
    globalized communication, 4
    militarized, 121
    of rights, 95
    secular, 12–13
    world risk, 69
soul, 42, 54, 67, 116, 134–35
    passions of, 103
    therapy of, 75
subjectivity, 11, 35, 38, 41, 52, 66,
    71, 84, 95, 106, 164
    crisis of, 114–15, 118, 137–38
    modern, 7, 14, 51, 91, 117
    See also Self
suicide, 147, 153

T
Taoism, 85, 136
technique/technology, 121–24, 127–
    28, 131–33, 135, 160
    and enframing, 126
    essence of, 126
    ethics of, 129–30
    and nihilism, 125, 136, 139
theology, 1, 17, 93
    theological origins of nihilism,
        5–6

Costantino Esposito is professor of history of philosophy and history of metaphysics at University of Bari Aldo Moro and at the Institute of Philosophical Studies of the Università della Svizzera Italiana (USI) in Lugano. He is the author of many books and articles, including *Introduzione a Heidegger*.

www.ingramcontent.com/pod-product-compliance
Lightning Source LLC
Chambersburg PA
CBHW060338100426
42812CB00003B/1035